The Crafty Entrepreneur

The Crafty Entrepreneur

Your guide to selling artwork and crafts online

DOUG MAXWELL

For my Mother

CONTENTS

ACKNOWLEDGMENTS

Little of merit is created in a vacuum.
I wish to thank the many people that contributed to the creation of this book. I especially thank the artists and crafters who offered insight through their own experiences. Thank you to Sarah for coordinating interviews and production without which this book would not have materialized. Thank you to Ginger and Ruth for their inspiration. And, finally thank you to Christopher for continual support.

1 INTRODUCTION

You are creative.

You make amazing things.

You want the joy of earning a living doing what you love, turning your craft that is your passion into a career. But how successful can you be by taking this journey outside the bounds of traditional corporate employment? In today's marketplace – very.

The Internet has made it possible for artists, crafters, photographers, writers and other creative folk to earn real livings doing what they love. In fact, there is an increasing demand for unique and creative items that are not mass produced. This appreciation for handmade items and artistic creations makes it possible for you to start your own business, online. Whether you are an Internet novice or an e-comm veteran, simple but proven keys to business and online promotion can turn your entrepreneurial dreams into reality.

Even in the midst of the recent economic downturn, Jackie Kaufman, jewelry artist and owner of Rock My World, left her retail shop and started selling her jewelry exclusively online. She found that despite being located in the major tourist destination of Fort Lauderdale, Florida, after paying rent and utilities, her brick-and-mortar store wasn't resulting in a profit. She realized that by moving her business online, she could reach a larger audience and sell more of her silver-cast jewelry.

But with the staggering statistics indicating that more online business start-ups fail than succeed, jumping into the waters of entrepreneurialism can be scary. Not to mention that stomach-churning fear that most creative, right-brain thinkers feel when they hear the word "business" or look at a financial statement.

Don't be intimidated. It's true; starting a creative business selling your craft isn't a get-rich-quick scheme. If you want to succeed, you'll need three main ingredients: inspiration, determination and a willingness to learn the keys that every crafty entrepreneur needs to know.

This may seem simple, but these are your keys to success regardless of your craft. My story's not so different from yours. I have spent years serving the Fortune 500 in corporate career assistance software. And, while I've helped thousands architect their own career moves, I've been left with a creative void of my own. Much like yours, I guess. After a realization that I could leverage what I learned helping others with their corporate careers, I decided to shift focus to you, to me, to the creative entrepreneurs.

KEYS TO SUCCESS

- **Stay Inspired**

- **Work Hard**

- **Keep Learning**

There's a lot to learn, but don't be discouraged. This book was written for you – to help you navigate the waters of entrepreneurialism and prepare you with the tools necessary to make your creative business a success.

This book is filled with information, tips and techniques I have learned over many years as a successful Internet entrepreneur. It is intended to serve as a comprehensive guide to the many different steps you will need to consider in order to make your creative business a success. We will discuss techniques to learn more about yourself, the basics of starting a business, specifics of a creative business, and of course selling and promotion online.

As you get started on your own business journey, I invite you to join us in our own creative community at Originl.com. Originl is a source of ongoing ideas and learning as creative folk share their inspiration and creations. Join to create your own portfolio site, share ideas, ask questions, find amazing things, and sell what you create. See the very back of this book for a special invitation and offer.

If this has you sitting up in your chair and intrigued, this book is for you. Here's a sneak peek of what you will learn in the chapters of this book.

The Creative Mind – The creative mind works differently than others; you are full of ideas. Embrace the creative thinking that makes you different and learn how to foster innovation and harness your creative bursts to work for you, not against you, as you create your business and your products.

Being Your Own Boss – When you plunge into the world of entrepreneurialism, you become the boss. Sure, not having a boss sounds nice, but being your own boss means you will be ultimately responsible for every task and decision necessary to run your business. Until you can afford to outsource some of those responsibilities, you will have to learn how to avoid distractions and fight procrastination so you can keep your business moving forward and find a healthy balance between your business and personal life.

About the Product – Your passion lies in creating, but you may or may not know what specific item you want to focus on and if it will be a profitable product. Do some brainstorming and some research on what other crafters are marketing, and then fine-tune your products to ensure success when you start selling. Stay flexible, and you will narrow in on the perfect niche product.

Building a Brand – Building a brand for your creative small business begins with determining a vision for your business. Decide what it is that you are about, what moves you. Then create a name that paints an image of your business and products. Take time to define the vision and mission for your business and seek feedback from friends and family to come up with a strong concept that will help you build a successful brand.

Strategic Planning for Creatives – With a vision, product and name in place, you're probably anxious to start selling. But first coming up with goals and a plan of action for your business can make all the difference in your success. Your plan is your roadmap detailing what you need to do to make your business adventure a success. Chart a destination, set a course and be prepared to check your map often.

Legal Considerations – We will discuss key topics to consider in regards to becoming an officially licensed business and protecting your unique products against unlawful reproduction. The type of business structure you choose and how you protect your creative intellectual property may not seem relevant in the early days of your business, but it's important to consider these things from the beginning. Trademarks, copyrights and patents are important even in small businesses.

Finances and Record-keeping –– Keeping meticulous records of business expenses, income and which items sell probably isn't your idea of a fun day at work. However, records are important for filing your personal or business taxes as well as monitoring how your business is growing. When you have accurate records to reference, you can make informed decisions on how to improve your products and raise your profit margin. We will cover proven and painless techniques to accomplish this.

Pricing Your Creations – You cannot expect to turn a profit by under-cutting your product prices to compete with similar mass-produced items. Your products are handmade, unique and infused with your creativity and personality. This makes them worth more than manufactured items. To decide how much you're going to charge for your creations, you'll need to consider many different factors.

Selling Online – Forget the days of dealing with a landlord or realtor to find a location for your business. Today, an online shop is a low-cost and prime piece of business realty. But where in cyberspace should you set up shop? We will discuss several popular venues to help you determine what's right for you.

Online Selling Tips – It's not enough to just snap quick photos of your products and list them in your online store. To make the most of your brand and get potential buyers engaged and excited about your products, you need to take high-quality photos of your products and write product descriptions that entice your customers to buy. If your product is functional, a demonstrational video will also help your customers get all the information they need to decide to make a purchase.

Marketing - Creating Demand – If you build it, they will come.. maybe. You may think it's hard to create demand for your creative business, especially considering how your prices compare to mass-merchandized items. But, thanks to the "Handmade Movement" in recent years, people are losing interest in mass-produced goods and going gaga over handcrafted creations. However, you will still have to generate a buzz about your business and products by getting your customers passionate about what you do. This is marketing; I will show you how with effective techniques for the newbie or veteran.

Be Found Online – You don't want to spend all your time finding your clients and delivering your marketing messages, so help your customers find you by building an online presence for your business. Create a website and blog for your business and learn how to use keywords to generate more traffic to your website that can translate to more sales.

Promoting Your Business Online – Today's Web is about more than just search engines. Once you have a website, blog and shop you've got to start promoting your business and products to generate visitors and readers that you can turn into buyers. To do this, you can write guest posts for other craft blogs and introduce yourself to a community within your target market. Additionally, you can list your business in key online directories to help local consumers find you online.

Networking and Social Media – These days everyone is communicating online, and that "everyone" includes folks in your target market. So, jump online and start talking about your creations. Make a social media profile, or several, for your business and start engaging in relevant conversations with your fans and followers. Make friends with potential customers and other artists or crafters. Build business connections so you can generate interest in your products and draw more visitors and potential buyers to your shop, website and blog. This is about engagement.

Promoting Your Business Offline – Help your products reach a larger audience by logging out of the virtual world and giving some traditional marketing strategies a try. Attend and sell at craft fairs, hand out business cards, write press releases to local newspapers, submit your products for inclusion in the appropriate magazines and sell your products in brick-and-mortar stores to reach more customers and generate more sales. An online + offline strategy is most powerful in building your brand.

Building Relationships with Buyers – Relationships are key. Make your marketing and networking efforts pay off by building relationships with existing and potential buyers. When you take time to engage in conversation on social media sites and chat with your buyers at craft fairs, you let your customers know that they are more than just dollar signs. This will ultimately result in more sales. Keep the conversation going before and after the sale so your buyers will retain interest in your business and products and share your information with their friends.

Advertising and Affiliates – Advertising is another great way to generate traffic to your online shop and website. You may place traditional offline ads in newspapers, local or trade magazines or purchase air time from local television and radio stations. However, you can often save money and set an ad budget that fits your needs – and reach a larger audience – by advertising online and using affiliates to advertise your products. There are many options; let's explore them.

Payment and Shipping – As you close sales, you will need sound options for payment and shipping. Thanks to a couple of popular online services and applications, you can accept various forms of payment whether you are selling in an online shop or in-person. When it is time to ship your creations out to buyers, charge reasonable shipping rates as necessary, to ensure your customers receive their products on time and in top condition.

Customer Service – No one wants to be mediocre. Turn your buyers into repeat customers by offering outstanding customer service. Go out of your way to make sure your customers are happy, even if that means sending replacement items or accepting refunds for your products. They will remember your thoughtfulness and talk up your business to their friends. The name of the game is quality in all that you do.

Taking the Next Step – If you follow these key steps, focus on a great product, and work hard, it will not take long for your business to start growing. When business starts booming, you may need to look into hiring full or part time employees and outsourcing some responsibilities. It may even be time to look into expanding your marketing, getting health insurance for your employees and restating your business's goals. However high you wish to climb, the key principles we will discuss in this book will help you get there.

Whether you are looking to make a little extra money from your part-time craft, turn your hobby into a full-time business, or expand your existing art or craft business, this book is for you. We'll discuss key steps and tactics to turn your creative passion into business success. You too can be, The Crafty Entrepreneur.

2 THE CREATIVE MIND

You are different. Creative people are different. By now, you've realized that – and not because scientific research has proven it, but because you have lived it. Through your education and throughout your career, I'm sure you have discovered that you think differently than most. You have probably spent a lot of time daydreaming and coming up with innovative and creative solutions for school and work projects. And you continue to generate new ideas constantly, drawing inspiration from everyone and everything around you – even drawing creative inspiration from strange places and situations that may seem weird to others.

In fact, your mind is a spring of ideas. You likely have a vast collection of ideas for creative products to make and sell, and you probably come up with new ideas every day.

But this abundance of ideas can also present a challenge. When ideas are flowing, possibly too many ideas, it may be difficult to follow through on any one to a successful end. Your creative energy may also refuse to yield to a work schedule. So, sometimes your idea spring bountifully pours out ideas while other times only a few ideas will trickle out. At times you can energetically burn the midnight oil while working on an exciting new idea, while other times you cannot seem to summon up a single useful thought. Plus, there's never a guarantee that

9

the ideas you treasure the most will turn out successful or profitable. This does not mean you should quickly jump to each new idea. Instead, you need to learn how to foster your creative bursts and test the waters on each idea to distinguish which ideas have merit and which are best to set aside.

Learn to foster your creative bursts and get those ideas flowing by looking for inspiration. Think about the locations and activities that help you come up with new ideas. Does browsing the Internet looking at photos inspire you? Or maybe sitting in the local park? Taking a walk through the historic district of your town? A local art museum? Poetry readings? Or perhaps you like to people-watch on a busy street or at your local shopping center?

When your pool of ideas seems stagnant, unclog your creative spring by engaging in those activities and visiting those places that inspire you. Observe the beauty in the world around you and even look at other creative products to spur new ideas to life.

As you stimulate the flow of your creative juices, try creating an inspiration album or sketch journal full of clippings, notes and drawings to keep your ideas collectively organized. You can also keep your brainstorms organized by pinning photo clips, sketches and notes onto a corkboard on the wall in your office. The point is, simply to keep your ideas together and store them for future use, so that you can stay focused on your current projects and have an easy-to-access organized collection to look at when you're ready to move to a new project.

When you have a new idea that you find especially exciting, it can be very tempting to skip ahead and leave behind unfinished projects that have become too dull and work-like. This is a common challenge creatives face. But do not so quickly abandon your old project. Instead, work to stay organized and follow-through on each of your ideas until you can determine if that idea is a profitable product to add to your portfolio or a misfire.

Success in a creative business is as much hard work, "perspiration" as the saying goes, as it is inspiration. I know how exciting it is to focus on ideation and brainstorming the next great creation, but it is the follow-through with those ideas that can separate you and your business from others. This makes all the difference. Remember that you do not always need to know all the actions that are required ahead to successfully bring your idea to fruition. What's important is to keep moving forward and continue taking the next step. This is the mark of an entrepreneur.

This doesn't mean that you need to follow-through on every idea you have. As some ideas sit you may realize that they will not fit your vision, your brand, or that they really were not such golden ideas after all. But with each new idea you pursue, look to your friends, family and the creative community to offer constructive feedback on your ideas. Above all, do not get discouraged if the feedback does not resonate the same thrill for your idea. It is much better to realize this early, before you invest too much time and energy trying to sell products that do not have a commercial appeal.

We understand how your creativity works, so at originl.com we've tailored our website to offer features you can use to harness your creative bursts and stay inspired using the help of your creative community. Through the use of Originl's inspiration albums you can collect online bookmark clippings of photos that inspire you and journal about your ideas to seek creative and constructive feedback from a community of fellow crafty entrepreneurs and potential buyers.

Know Yourself

The chapters ahead cover a very broad range of business topics and techniques for successful selling online. But first, it's important to know yourself. My years of experience in corporate career development have solidified the importance of introspection prior to major career events. Take a moment, or longer, to complete the following thinking exercise as a starting point for your journey.

First, think about the things in life you enjoy most. These can be jobs, college courses, hobbies or anything really that you absolutely love doing. If helpful, write these down. Now, limit this list to just those activities that really fulfill you. Leave out things that are fun but not totally fulfilling to the point you enjoy doing them repeatedly and seriously.

Think about what it is about these activities that draw you in. Are there any common themes in these jobs or activities? Try to distill down to the core functions that you are most passionate about. Is it creating, working with your hands or in solitude? Is it surrounding yourself with beauty or maybe the praise you receive from others? Possibly it is troubleshooting or finding solutions to challenges. Whatever commonalities you find, remember them as they are keys to your professional happiness.

Next, think about your ideal work environment. Visualize if it is a bright open space or a cozy tungsten lit studio. Are there other people around to give you feedback and advice, or is it your own domain with solitude from which you draw energy? These are clues to where you will be most effective, successful and happy. While there's no right or wrong in this exercise, it's important to understand how you are energized and draw inspiration.

Finally, consider what you value most. What are your core values as a person that are most important in both personal and professional situations. Innovation, humor, social responsibility, financial freedom? Again, any answer can be correct.

What did you learn from this exercise? Likely there are no dramatic surprises but possibly some unexpected realizations. Use what you learned about yourself, remember it, and let it guide you in your entrepreneurial adventure ahead.

3 BEING YOUR OWN BOSS

The thought of being your own boss is a romanticized idea. You don't have to deal with office politics or worry constantly about what your superiors think of your on-the-job performance. There's not a time clock to punch or vacation request form to be approved. But, at the same time you've got a lot more responsibilities when you become your own boss. It's important to recognize this early on.

In actuality, being your own boss can often be a lot harder on creative folk. As a creative, you want to concentrate on making your artwork or craft, not tracking sales reports, performing market research, recording placed orders, packaging orders or dealing with the shipping process. But, if you want to make your own business a reality, you have to do those left-brain duties too, especially if you are going it alone.

With so many responsibilities, time is of utmost importance. When you're not working, you're not making money. And if you're not using your time wisely, you will end up spending all your evenings and weekends doing makeup work instead of getting to enjoy more time with your family, which is likely one reason why you decided to be your own boss in the first place.

To keep your business profitable and your work enjoyable, you'll need to learn how to schedule your time wisely, stay focused and avoid distractions without stifling the creative process. The good news is, it can be done! In this chapter, we will discuss key challenges and simple straightforward approaches to being your own boss.

Fighting Procrastination

When you're in business for yourself, procrastination is your most formidable enemy. As a creative person, you have a tendency to procrastinate those tedious business tasks that you may not really want to do in the first place. But, when you start procrastinating, you eat away at time you planned to use brainstorming or creating amazing things. By following a scheduled routine, you can zap procrastination and use your time wisely.

Use the following tips to fight procrastination and create a schedule that caters to your needs.

> **TIP**
>
> If you're fortunate enough to have a business partner, you can follow the example of Kevin and Shawn Hull, owners and artists at Hull's Happiest Days Designs, who split their business responsibilities to give each other more time to devote to creating.

Track Your Time

To help you stay on task and meet deadlines, begin by tracking how you spend your time so that you can formulate a schedule that gives you enough time to finish all the tasks you need to do each day. Jessica Partain, co-owner and artist at Inedible Jewelry admits that she compulsively tracks how she spends her time. As a result, she knows exactly how long it should take her to perform each of her usual daily business duties, in addition to how long it takes her to make the polymer clay food-shaped charms her shop is known for. Tracking your time is also very important when pricing your products. We'll discuss this more later on.

Realize You Need a Flexible Schedule

By knowing how much time it takes you to finish each of your business or creative duties when you're not distracted or procrastinating, you can begin to formulate a schedule that will help you stay on task. However, do not think of a schedule as a strict outline of your day. Some tasks like checking email, responding to customers on social media and dealing with shipping problems will pop up unexpectedly and take up extra time in your day. Realize that you're not always going to be able to clock out after putting in 8 hours, nor do you need to. Developing a schedule is a tool to help you, not constrict you.

Write Down a List of Priority To-Dos

One of the most simple techniques in time management is also one of the most effective. At the end of each work day, prepare for the next by writing down two or three things you need to focus your efforts on the following day. When the next morning arrives, devote your attention to completing first those tasks on your priority list and the focus you summon for those tasks will likely stick with you for the rest of your workday. Don't be overwhelmed at the thought you must create an extensive list. Simply write down the next action and keep your to-do lists moving forward.

Reward Yourself

Keep yourself motivated to follow through on your responsibilities by rewarding yourself for even minor victories. Each morning, agree to give yourself a reward only if you finish all tasks on your priority to-do list. Rewards can be as simple as ordering a book off Amazon or heading to the local café for a delicious afternoon treat.

Change Your Work Environment

When you find yourself repeatedly procrastinating the non-creative duties of owning your own business, try changing your work environment when working on those tasks. Laura Kelly, stained glass artist and owner of peaceloveglass, often leaves her in-home workspace and heads to her local library, café or a shared work space to take care of business tasks. She claims she can concentrate better on her business responsibilities when she's not sitting in her home studio environment.

Give this a try, and even if you don't get as much work done as anticipated, the change of scenery and chance to communicate with others may give you a spark of energy and inspiration that you can use to get more work done when you get home.

However, procrastination can also happen when you don't know what the logical next step is. Even if the next step is not monumental, it is important to always keep moving forward. Look for the "Take Action!" steps at the end of this chapter and throughout this book to get your business headed in the right direction.

> QUOTE
>
> *"Being your own boss is hard; it's hard because your success is directly correlated to how much time and effort you put into your business."*
>
> - Caitlin McNamara, owner and designer at Moxie & Oliver

Avoiding Distractions

A close contender, distractions are often just as detrimental to your productivity as procrastination. When unimportant distractions are taking up too much of your time, you're not getting your business and creating responsibilities taken care of.

When you work from home, you often encounter more distractions than when you work outside the home. This often occurs because you now have to find a way to balance your work and personal life. Tending to small children, taking family members to doctor's appointments and carpooling to and from school can distract you from work responsibilities and get your mind out of focus-mode. It's easy to get distracted by your home environment, friends, pets or worst of all television.

Even though you do not have a boss staring over your shoulder, you must be conscientious of how you spend your time. And while these personal distractions may make working at home a less lonely job, they can significantly draw your attention away from what you should be focusing on.

You can also become distracted by stress and worrying over the length of your to-do list. Remind yourself to not fall into this trap. Never forget to relish in the joy of owning your own business and creating what you love most. This is your dream, and it's starting to become a reality!

While distractions can come from anywhere to sabotage your productivity, the following are a few easy solutions you can use to stay on-task during the workday.

Turn off the television

I know it can get lonely working by yourself or from your home, but if you're spending more time looking at your television than chipping away at your business duties, then it's time to grab the clicker and turn that contraption off. At the very least, turn your television around so you can continue to draw inspiration from the storylines, news or music while preventing yourself from constantly looking up from your work.

Turn on some music

If you prefer some ambient noise to silence, try listening to your radio or some of your favorite inspirational music. Consider trying out an online music service like Pandora.com which can model your musical tastes and keep a stream of music flowing into your home office or studio without the need to flip through your iPod or CDs or listen to radio commercials.

Alexandra Koiv metal sculpting artist and owner of Alex in Welderland's Custom Pet Urns is a big fan of playing music while she works. She says that music helps distract her mind from worrying about how much work she has to do. This helps her enjoy the process of creating her pieces.

Avoid personal calls during work hours

Let your friends and family know when your usual work hours are and ask them not to disturb you by calling or stopping by during those hours. If you find yourself working extra hours, just ignore your personal calls and let your answering machine or caller ID be your secretary. You can return those calls when you're not working.

Take an in-house retreat

Try locking yourself in your home office, studio or workshop for a day or an entire weekend to catch up on work, stock up on pieces for your busy seasons or just to get some uninterrupted work time. Send your kids to their grandparents or hire a sitter and kiss your spouse goodbye for the day. Give yourself some solitude to get your creativity out and discover creative solutions to those challenging business issues.

Use timers and deadlines to stay focused

Sometimes working under pressure can be very motivating. Try using timers to keep your mind focused on important tasks. Using the

Pomodoro Technique (www.pomodorotechnique.com), you can set a timer to 25 minutes, or any other time-increment that suits your needs, and spend that time fully devoted to a specific task such as record-keeping or packaging orders to ship. When the timer goes off, take a 5 or 10 minute break or work on a smaller task, like checking email or updating your social media profiles. Then, re-set the timer for another period of uninterrupted work. Working under the pressure of a timer or impending deadline is a good technique to establish mini goals, so you won't be tempted to procrastinate during that time or allow yourself to get distracted by commenting on friend's photos on Facebook.

Software and Apps for Productivity

Aside from the Pomodoro Technique, there are other computer programs, smart phone applications and services you can use to help you track your time and stay on task. The creatives that helped with this book recommended the following programs.

Harvest (www.getharvest.com) is software you can use to track your project time, organize sales and quickly invoice online. Additionally, you can view reports to help you track earnings, stay on budget and make informed decisions that better fit your business and help your business grow.

Freedom (www.macfreedom.com) is a productivity app you can use on your Windows or Mac computer to block yourself from using your Internet connection for a period of up to 8 hours, so you can avoid checking your personal social media profiles and stay focused on business-related tasks.

Self-Control (hwww.macupdate.com/app/mac/31289/selfcontrol) is similar to Freedom, but offers the added benefit of allowing you to block yourself from visiting specific websites and mail servers, so that you can still use the Internet but can lock yourself out of attention consuming websites during work time.

Although being your own boss is hard work and requires self-discipline, it is often the most rewarding career decision you can make. When you become your own boss, you can control how you spend your energy, define your own company policies and find a schedule that suits your creativity. Plus, you no longer have to deal with a day job that drains your creativity or a work environment that does not support and foster your creative mind.

Take Action!

☑ **Set up a work space in your home.**

Instead of trying to run your business out of your living room, give yourself an office or work shop. This way, you can shut your door to avoid distractions like the television, family members/roommates and those household chores you try to justify as allowable distractions. Also, by setting up your own private workstation, you don't have to feel guilty about your creative messes and you can make space for a bulletin board to gather inspirational ephemera.

☑ **Remove distractions from your workspace.**

Hooked on a video game or daytime television? Get rid of everything in your workspace that distracts you from what you should be working on.

☑ **Hire a sitter.**

Being able to spend more time with your children is a wonderful benefit to being your own boss. However, you know your kids can be a handful sometimes. When your budget allows, hire a sitter for one or two days a week so you can have extra time to take care of business. If you can't hire a sitter, see if your spouse, friends, siblings or parents care to take the kids for a couple of hours once or twice a week so you can get some extra work done.

4 ABOUT THE PRODUCT

What are you going to sell?

By now I know you are getting excited about the prospect of turning your passion into a career. The next step is deciding what you are going to sell. Maybe you already have something in mind or maybe you are still not clear on what you want to make. Either way, it's time to start doing a little brainstorming so that you can pick a craft that fits your interests and talents and find a way to make your product unique.

Begin by identifying your key talents -- those creative hobbies you can turn into a steady income. Are you a painter? Do you take amazing photos? Do you like to make jewelry? Key chains? Pins? Or maybe you like to sew? Or crochet? Think about your recent creative passion as well as the artwork or crafts you have made since childhood. Sisters Jessica and Susan Partain at Inedible Jewelry started making polymer clay trinkets as children and eventually turned that treasured childhood pastime into a successful business.

However, there is no rule that says you have to choose a craft you are familiar with. Do some soul-searching and find a craft you are interested in learning about and feel you will retain interest in. You may even be able to find a way to transform an existing art form into something truly one-of-a-kind. That is exactly what artists and husband-and-wife team, Kevin and Shawn Hull did with their shop, Hull's Happiest Days Designs. Though both Kevin and Shawn are sketch artists, they made their products unique by investing nearly five months of their time learning the process they now use to transfer their designs onto fine china dinner ware.

Maybe you have an idea for a craft you are passionate about, but your idea isn't brand new; there are other creative businesses out there already doing what you want to do. Don't let that be a road block. Use your creative mind to figure out a way to take an existing design and make it your own.

Don't just re-do what someone else is doing and offer your products at a lower price; that's no way to run a business. Besides being ethically questionable, if you are undercutting someone else's prices, you are probably not going to make enough money to justify the time you spend making the pieces. You'll only attract bargain-hunters, not customers happy to pay the prices you should be charging for original handmade products.

As you continue to brainstorm what you can create and sell, Jackie Kaufman at Rock My World recommends that you seek "the sticky factor". By this she means that you want to create a unique product that makes people say, "oh, I've never saw that before" and then you are going to stick in their minds and be there when they have extra cash to spend, or need a one-of-a-kind gift for a friend or loved one.

In design, I've heard this referenced as your "zebra". Why zebra? Well, a horse without stripes is just a horse, but one with the unique black and white markings of a zebra make it incredibly memorable. When creating your art or designs, think what it is that makes them unique. What's your zebra?

Most importantly, do not pick a craft just because you think it will be profitable. Choose something you are passionate about. If you don't, you will have trouble generating new ideas and you will quickly lose interest in your new career path. How can you expect your customers to be passionate about what you are doing, if you're not?

This is your opportunity to take an amazing turn in your career; do not take it lightly.

Fine-Tuning Your Product

Once you have decided what you want to sell, have learned how to create it, and before you ever list the first piece in an online shop, make several varieties and ask your friends and family for feedback. Give away a few items to test their quality and durability, if applicable, and post images of your creations on your Facebook page to get feedback from your peers. Use this feedback to improve your product, as necessary, so that you can produce the highest quality products for your customers. Don't have a Facebook page? No worries, we'll soon discuss how to set one up. You can even ask your friends for their input on what prices you should charge, but we will talk more about that in the Pricing Your Creations chapter later in this book.

> ## JARGON ALERT
>
> If you want to get technical about it, getting feedback on your products from potential customers is a business tactic known as **market research**.

The range of creative products that can be successful is unlimited. Here is a gallery of some example creative designs that sell. What is common to each is not a specific craft or style, but the uniqueness and quality that comes with a handmade creative item. As you browse, think about what makes them unique.

Pink Birthday Cake Slice Necklace – Jessica and Susan Partain, Inedible Jewelry

Bacon and Eggs Earrings – Jessica and Susan Partain, Inedible Jewelry

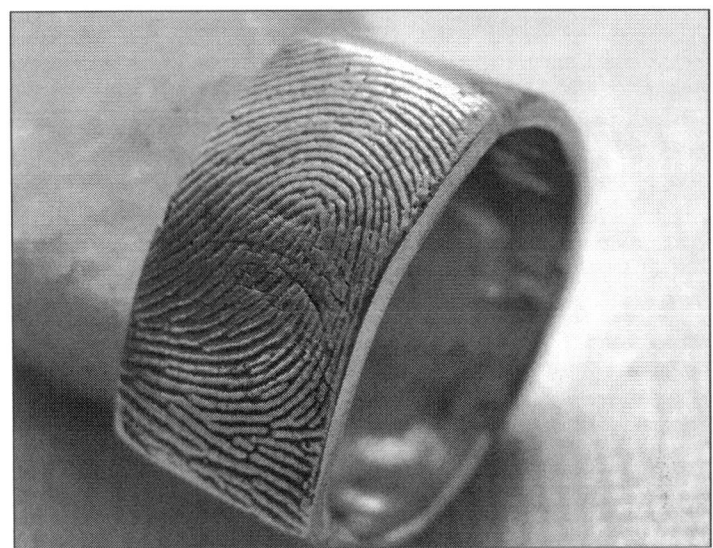

Fingerprint Wedding Band Ring – Jackie Kaufman, Rock My World

Fingerprint Puzzle Necklace – Jackie Kaufman, Rock My World

Backpack – Heather Valentine, The Sewing Loft

Quirky Dolls – Heather Valentine, The Sewing Loft

Apple Tree Folk Plates – Kevin & Shawn Hull, Hull's Happiest Days Designs

Ice Cream Man Mug – Kevin & Shawn Hull, Hull's Happiest Days Designs

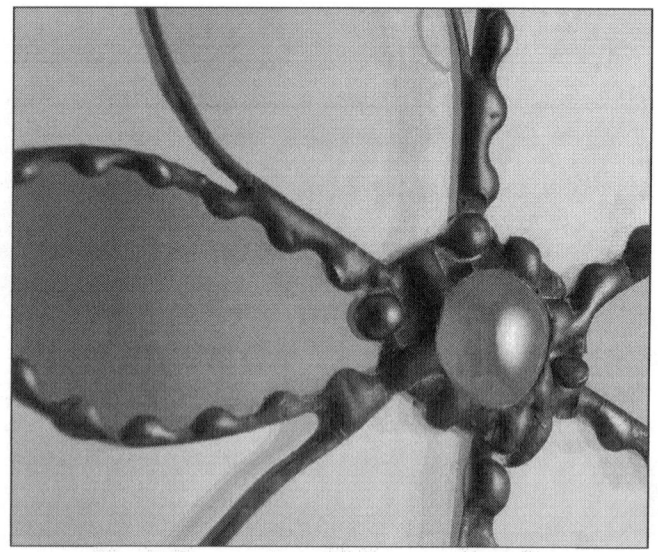

Hippie Flower – Laura Kelly, peaceloveglass

Woodstock – Laura Kelly, peaceloveglass

My Old Kentucky Home Quilt – Debbie Stephens

Camo Frog Baby Quilt – Pamela Walter

Woods Colt Painting – David Roger Davis

Carolina Wren Wood Carving – Mark Eclov

Miniature China Cabinet – Doug Doerrfeld

Rocking Chair Gourd – Linda Harse-Lancette

Finger Puppets – Stacey Rebecca Gordon, Puppet Pie

Finger Puppet – Stacey Rebecca Gordon, Puppet Pie

Feather Earrings – Lauren Killbourne, The Littlest Feather

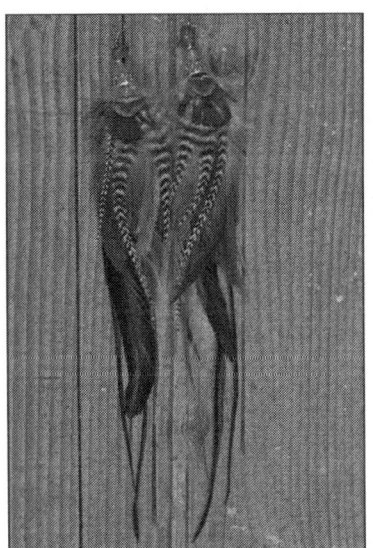

Feather Earrings – Lauren Killbourne, The Littlest Feather

Finding Wholesale Supplies

Buying your art or crafting supplies from a local craft store can drive your expenses up. Don't get me wrong, local craft shops are great for the hobbyist crafter, or for picking up supplies when you're in a pinch. But you will be spending a lot of money on supplies, so why not get the best deal on your materials?

To get more bang for your business's buck, search out wholesale suppliers so you can increase your profit margin. Wholesale suppliers offer lower prices and bulk quantities of supplies, though you may have to research several different suppliers and make price comparisons to find the best deal on the quality supplies you use to create your crafty products.

We have collected a starter list of wholesale suppliers you can reference at the end of this book to begin your research. However, you can locate additional wholesale suppliers by heading to your favorite search engine and searching for general suppliers using the keywords "wholesale craft suppliers". Additionally, you can find wholesale suppliers in your specific industry by searching for those suppliers using such keyword searches as: "wholesale ribbon suppliers", "clay wholesale suppliers" or "doll making wholesale supplies". Just insert your craft supply or craft industry into the search engine with the keywords "wholesale supplies" or "wholesale suppliers" and begin comparing prices to find the suppliers that offer you the best deals.

Create a spreadsheet or document on your computer to keep track of which suppliers offer which deals. You may have to use different suppliers to get better quality or deals on various items, or you may want to switch suppliers during different seasons to take advantage of special deals or sales.

Wholesale suppliers are not the only place to get great deals on supplies. Stay on the lookout and you could luck into an amazing deal on supplies from an unconventional source.

Here are a few recommendations from other artists and crafters.

Laura Kelly, owner of peaceloveglass, recommends checking Craigslist (www.craigslist.com) for people giving away art and craft supplies.

Heather Valentine, owner and designer at The Sewing Loft is keen on being green, so she often buys fabric second-hand at yard sales. Sometimes she'll bring home an old dress with a funky pattern just because it inspires her. She is also fond of gathering scrap fabric that fabric producers cut off the edges and ends of fabric rolls.

Lauren Kilbourne, jewelry artist and owner of The Littlest Feather often trades a free pair of earrings for supplies from other jewelry artists she networks with.

Take Action!

☑ **Learn your trade.**

It's okay if you're a novice. Everyone has to start somewhere. However, if you want to improve, learn all you can about your trade including new techniques and methods. Buy books and magazines in your specific craft industry, watch free instructional videos online, read blogs and articles online and find other crafters in your medium that are willing to give you advice and answer your questions. Learning about your trade helps you improve your products so you have a better product and more referrals from happy buyers.

☑ **Research wholesale suppliers.**

Find wholesale suppliers that offer the items you need to create your products. You may have to locate more than one supplier to satisfy all your needs. Create a spreadsheet or list to organize available suppliers and compare the prices each wholesale supplier charges in order to find the best deals for your business. Add web address links

(URLs) to your list or spreadsheet so you can quickly locate supplies when you need to restock your inventory.

5 BUILDING A BRAND

Branding, by definition and relevance to the crafty entrepreneur, is the product identity and personality with which you market your business and creative products. The goal is to have a clear brand identity and to leave a lasting impression on your customers.

To start defining your brand think back to what makes you and your product unique. What is special, memorable or your specific niche? If you were at a dinner party and someone asked you what you create, consider how you would answer in a single sentence. This is the starting point for your brand.

What's In a Name?

Your shop's name is often your potential customers' first impression of your business. So, it goes without saying that a good name helps you make a dynamite first impression. But coming up with a name is not always easy; you've got to figure out how to sum up what your business is all about in just a few words.

To help you find a name for your shop, I recommend the following strategy.

1.   Define Your Concept

Knowing what your business stands for can make the process of finding a name easier. Try writing out a sentence or two that sums up who you are and what you wish to accomplish with your business. Try completing the sentence "They are the people who…" with information about your business. For example, "They are the people who make amazing tea cozies out of recycled materials." or "That is the person who paints abstract, whimsical landscapes with watercolors."

> **SNEAK PEEK**
>
> We'll get into further detail about defining your business's vision and mission in the following chapter, Strategic Planning for Creatives.

2.   Brainstorm

Pull a blank sheet of paper out of your printer or notebook and start writing down a list of words that relate to you and your business. Then, write down a list of words that describe your business's mission. Expand the list by considering words that describe your design aesthetic, technique or even color palette. Finally, write down a list of emotion words - like "happy", "love", "warm", "friendly", "comfort" - that you think accurately portray the image you want to create for your business; use your thesaurus to explore this final list further.

Once you're done with those first three lists, start combining words from each list to create potential names for your business. Jot down another list of the combinations you create that appeal to you on first impression. Rhymes are often used in word combinations.

As you've noticed, names for online business are incredibly creative these days. These are typically referred to as Web 2.0 names. You can use techniques like blending, character replacement and misspelling if you're after a modern unique name.

Blending is an approach where you take two words and connect them by removing parts of one or both words. You can use this technique for fairly simple or dramatic blends and typically works best if the words share common characters. Character replacement can be used to create new novel words by replacing individual characters in dictionary words. Vowels are typically replaced with other vowels. Misspellings are more and more common these days as well and similar to character replacement. This approach is simply altering the spelling of words typically by removing vowels or duplicating characters. Results of these techniques can be fun or bizarre, so use wisely.

3.   Say Your Name Out Loud

Practice saying your potential business names out loud. Pretend you are saying your business name to customers at craft fairs, or talking about your business to someone you meet in line at the movies. Pretend you're answering your business's phone line. Are your potential names easy to pronounce? Say them out loud to friends; can they understand what you are saying and guess how to spell it?

4.   Seek Feedback

Bounce your name ideas off family and friends. Ask them to tell you why they like certain names more than others and if they think any specific names have the "sticky factor". Keep a tally of which names are more popular among those friends and family that fit into your target market of customers. In the end, your success will not depend solely on your business name, so don't stress and enjoy the process.

5.   Check for Availability

Once you have some ideas in mind, check to make sure there is not another business operating using that same name. If another business exists under the same name, make sure they do not reside within the same city or state as you and that they do not offer the same products you offer. You may also want to check to see if the name you have in mind is available as a website address as this may influence you to change your name so that your business name and website address are the same and therefore easy for customers to remember when looking you up online.

There are some great online tools to help with this process. Name Station (www.namestation.com), Make Words (www.makewords.com) and Name Boy (www.nameboy.com) are a few of my favorites. These can help you generate potential business names using the described techniques as well as find available matching domain names. This is important as you begin promoting your business online.

These are not the only strategies you can use to brainstorm your shop name. Here are a few examples of how some of your fellow crafty entrepreneurs came up with their shop names:

Lauren Kilbourne's jewelry shop, The Littlest Feather, combines her nickname among her friends, "Littlest" with the material she uses to create her beautiful jewelry pieces: feathers.

Laura Kelly drew inspiration from a song that meant a lot to her when she was switching careers to come up with the name of her shop, peaceloveglass. Although the song lyric that inspired her was actually "peace, love, free," she replaced the last word with glass, the material she uses to create her gorgeous suncatchers and figurines.

Alexandra Koiv had SEO and keywords in mind when she came up with her shop name: Alex in Welderland's Custom Pet Urns.

> **JARGON ALERT**
>
> SEO stands for search engine optimization and refers to the process of optimizing your shop, website and blog for search engines by using keywords or keyword phrases that your customers will use to find your shop and products when performing a search.

Nikki McGonigal felt that it was important to include her first name in the title of her business – Nikki, In Stitches. She says, "Part of what makes Nikki, In Stitches so special is the personal connection so many of my readers and fans have with me, so it makes sense that my name should be in the title."

Husband and wife team and owners of Hull's Happiest Days Designs, Kevin and Shawn Hull's creations are intended as keepsakes of important days in their customer's lives, that's why their business name includes the words "happiest days". Kevin and Shawn also included their surname in their business name to avoid additional filing fees associated with having a fictitious business name licensed in their home state.

Take Action

☑ **Determine your state's requirements for filing fictitious names.**

Different states have different laws in regard to operating your business under fictitious names, i.e. not your personal name. To determine the laws for your state, visit Register Your Fictitious or "Doing Business As" (DBA) Name on the U.S. Small Business Administration's website (http://www.sba.gov/content/how-name-business).

6 STRATEGIC PLANNING FOR CREATIVES

As a business owner, you need goals and a plan of action to achieve those goals. Maybe your goal is simply to make enough money with your creative business that you can escape your traditional job, or maybe you have another goal in mind. Whatever your target, goal setting is a vital part of starting your own business. Think of your goals as stops along the road toward your destination in your entrepreneurial journey. Without them, you may move along aimlessly without direction. With them, you'll have a clear path and measure for your success.

Setting SMART Goals

I recommend using the SMART method described ahead to define your goals. This is a proven business technique that is adapted to your creative venture. A SMART goal is an acronym for a goal that is Specific, Measurable, Attainable, Realistic and Timely. By setting a SMART goal, you can ensure that you set realistic goals you can easily track progress on and achieve in the time constraints you specify.

Use the following checklist template to define your SMART goals. You may want to record these in a separate document so you can update your progress and make new goals as you achieve your targets.

Your Goal:

_____

_____

_____

Specific - You have a better chance of accomplishing your goals if they are specific and not general.

To make your goal as specific as possible, answer the following questions:

1.   What do you want to accomplish?

2.   What is the purpose or expected outcome of accomplishing that goal?

3.   By what date do you want to accomplish your goal?

4.   What tools or services will you require to accomplish your goal by your deadline?

5.   What problems could arise that would prevent you from accomplishing your goal on time?

Measurable - When you can track progress on your goals and see your achievements, you will stay motivated to reach your goal. A goal that cannot be measured is difficult to know when achieved.

To help you set a measurable goal, consider the following questions:

1. What factors or data can you use to track progress on your goals?

2. How will you know when your goal is accomplished?

Attainable - Coming up with an attainable goal is tricky. While you want to make sure that you can meet your goals by deadline, you also want to avoid setting goals that are too easy to reach. A goal that pushes you beyond what you already know you can accomplish helps you improve your work ethic and guarantees that you stay motivated to fulfilling that goal. However, if you set unrealistic goals, you're only setting yourself up for failure and giving yourself an extra helping of stress.

To ensure your goal is attainable and keeps you moving forward, ask yourself the following questions:

1. Is this goal achievable in the time frame you have specified? If so, why do you feel that it is achievable?

2. Docs this goal push you to work harder and improve your productivity? Or will the extra work distract you from other responsibilities and overwhelm you?

3. What, if any, smaller steps will you need to complete in order to ensure you meet your goal in time?

Realistic - Similar to being attainable, your business goals should also be realistic to your abilities. A realistic goal is an objective YOU are both willing and able to work towards and accomplish. If you don't currently have the resources or skills to achieve this goal, consider an intermediate goal to attain those resources and then restate.

Use the following questions to ensure that your goal is realistic for you:

1. Do you possess the ability, skills and tools necessary to achieve your goal on time?

2. Will any of your other responsibilities compete for the time and attention you will need to accomplish your goal on time?

Timely - You can write down your lifetime goals all day. But, unless you set a time frame for reaching those goals, there will be no sense of urgency inspiring and driving you to work on your goals each day.

Answer the following questions to help set time constraints for completion of your goal:

1. Rethink your answer to the previous question, "By when do you want to accomplish your goal?" Is your answer to that question specific and realistic for your abilities?

2. Is there any special reason why you want to accomplish your goal by that date or in that time frame?

3. Does your deadline or time frame make you feel motivated or overwhelmed?

As you work to create goals for your creative business, think about what you want to accomplish during the first year your virtual doors are open (or during the coming year, if you are already an established business). Do you want to introduce a new product? Move to a new selling platform? Or do you aspire to turn a profit in your first year and pay back any loans or start-up expenses you may have incurred? Think, as well, about the things you need to do to generate more customers and in result more profit; things such as starting a blog, updating your website and coming up with money to invest in advertising.

Creating a Business Plan

Now that you've specified your business's goals and set motivational targets, it's time to generate a business plan. Before you panic at the thought of black and white financial statements and legal documents, know that business planning can be fun. A business plan helps you to focus your vision for the business and it's a necessary step in ensuring your business venture is successful.

And, unless you're in need of a start-up loan or looking for investors, you don't even need a formal business plan. However, you should at least come up with an informal plan that you can reference when making decisions to improve and guide your business forward.

This section covers key components of a business plan for a creative business. When

> **DISCLAIMER**
>
> A formal business plan requires more parts and more detail than what we have outlined in this book. So, if you are seeking investments or loans and need a formal business plan, it may be best to seek the counsel of an accountant or lawyer who can help you create a formal plan.

you first start filling out your business plan, you may have trouble completing all the parts. That's ok; your business plan will require a lot of tweaking during the first few years your business is in operation, so just plan to update your business plan often as additional information is available.

Use the following steps to begin creating your own creative business plan.

The Executive Summary

The executive summary should be quite short and introduce your business concept. It's not important to get into the details here, but instead simply state what your business is about. Refer back to the previous visioning exercise as the foundation.

1. Define your business vision and values.

It's helpful to include a vision statement in your executive summary. A vision statement is the inspiration, hopes and dreams of your business. It should paint a picture about where you are headed, but not necessarily how you will get there. Write a vision statement that defines the long-term goal you have for your business. Be sure to think far ahead, not just in the next year or two.

Your vision should also include references to your values as an organization. Consider which values are integral to that vision and will play an important role in future decisions you make for your business. Write down a list of those values you find most important. Examples include but are not limited to:

- Customer delight
- Sustainability
- Innovation
- Quality
- Humor
- Eco-friendly
- Passionate
- Social responsibility

Write down any additional values important to your business that will help you define your business' goals and vision.

2.   Write a mission statement for your business.

Next, state how you will achieve your vision. Your mission statement defines your business purpose and what you do. Answer the following questions to help formulate a statement – a few sentences in length – that summarizes the main points of your business.

- Who is your target audience or customer?
- What do you do?
- Why do you do it?
- What does your business stand for?

Company Overview

Now that you've briefly summarized your business vision and mission, describe in more detail what your business does. Include specifics on what products you will make and for what market. This is where you should also start to outline how you will sell them and how you expect to make a profit. It may be early on to have all the answers on how you will do this, that's what this book is for. However, start at least to outline your ideas on how you expect to turn your craft into a real business.

> **TIP**
>
> Don't claim to contribute a portion of your proceeds to charity as a means of increasing sales. Choose a specific charity that means something to you and let your customers know why that charity is important to you; this will help you build a relationship with your customers.

Competitive Analysis

3. Define your competition.

Conduct market research to determine who your competition is. Begin by searching for similar creative businesses through keyword searches on your favorite search engine such as Google. Then, visit ecommerce sites like Etsy (www.etsy.com), Ebay (www.ebay.com) and our own Originl community to see if you have competition in those places.

SNEAK PEEK

Conducting market research is an ongoing need. You will want to keep an eye on your competition throughout the lifetime of your business to monitor when you need to make improvements to your business practices and products.

Look at what your competition is doing, what products they're making and how they are building relationships with their customers. Determine what your competition is doing well that may give them an edge over you. But, always remember you are unique. There's no need to copy what your competitors do. The point here is to be informed and educated only to help you form your own direction.

4. Determine how you stand out from the competition.

As you examine your competition, think about how you differ from them and what makes you stand out from them in a positive way. If you cannot easily identify this now, how can you position yourself to differentiate or have an advantage over your competition? Can you offer a larger variety or maybe be more specialized? Is your technique somehow unique or individual to you? These will help you look different in the eyes of potential buyers.

Market Analysis

5.   Define your target market.

Think about the creative products you are offering and make a list of the general types of people that you feel your products appeal to. If you have already started selling online or off, think about the kinds of people that already purchase from you. While you will be surprised sometimes by customers that you don't expect to be interested in your products, by making generalizations about your target market you can tailor your marketing efforts to your ideal customers.

If you're having trouble defining who your target market includes, Jessica Partain at Inedible Jewelry recommends that you do a backwards process of elimination by specifying who your target market is not. Great tip!

Marketing Plan

6.   Write an action plan for getting the word out about your business.

Begin by determining the places online and off where you can market your business for free. If you have marketing funds available, determine additional marketing mediums, as applicable. Create a timing schedule for your marketing campaigns, as well as what messages you want to share to raise awareness about your business. Don't worry, this can be general at this stage. You

SNEAK PEEK

You will read more about creating demand in the Marketing, Promoting Yourself Online and Promoting Yourself Offline chapters to determine which marketing methods will best fit your target market.

can expand this further as you learn more about the marketing and promotion opportunities we will discuss in later chapters.

Financial Plan

7.   Forecast your business expenses and revenue.

Estimating the cost of your business expenses and how much you anticipate making from your business will help you determine an approximate profit margin. This can help you evaluate if the prices you intend to charge for your products will result in a profit after you deduct the cost of supplies and the overhead of running your business.

Determining a financial plan for your business may be easier to develop once you have been in business for a few months and have a better idea of where your money is being spent and how many sales you are making. You probably already have a price in mind for your creations and rough ideas as to costs involved. We will discuss this in more detail and help you fine tune your financial plan. In the beginning, make informed estimations and be prepared to update your financial plan often in the first few years your business is in operation.

Use the sample spreadsheet ahead to help you forecast your profit or loss from your business. This sample is intended to illustrate the key concepts of a financial plan. If you are creating a business plan for a bank loan or investment, consider consulting an accountant or business advisor for further assistance in financial planning.

	Yearly	January	February
Income			
From Product A	$	$	$
From Product B	$	$	$
Etc.	$	$	$
Total Income	$	$	$
Expenses			
Advertising	$	$	$
Auto expenses	$	$	$
Equipment	$	$	$
Internet hosting	$	$	$
Office supplies	$	$	$
Rent	$	$	$
Sales tax	$	$	$
Shipping costs	$	$	$
Utilities	$	$	$
Miscellaneous	$	$	$
Total Expenses	$	$	$
Profit or Loss (Total Income minus Total Expenses)	$	$	$

Unfortunately, it's not always this simple. As you grow, cash flow will become increasingly important to track, possibly even more important than revenue. A quick tip to managing the flow of cash in and out of your business is to determine what percentage of your revenue comes in within the first 30 days after your sale, next month and so on. If almost all is received within 30 days, your cash flow is roughly equal to the net revenue (profit/loss). If not, then multiple the total income per month by the percent received in that month, the next month, etc. This will help you get a better view of how much cash you will likely have on hand and forecast through busy seasons for buying supplies and selling your creations.

Management and Personnel Plan

8. Create your team.

You may not have employees to manage, but when you have more work than you can handle or a task to take care of that isn't in your list of skills, it's handy to have someone to turn to. Think about what projects you have coming up that you may need help with or need to learn more about. Reach out and build a business relationship with professionals that can help you with those projects and add their information to your contact list.

Your team may include other creative business owners that can offer advice on business-related issues such as mentors that can teach you more about your craft, accountants, web designers and even copywriters. This is one reason why networking and building relationships is so important.

> **TIP**
>
> Reach out to independent, freelance writers, website designers and even graphic designers that are willing to offer low-prices or free services in exchange for portfolio samples.

Don't feel you have to work in a bubble even though you own your own business. Nor should you feel you have to do everything. A mark of leadership is knowing when you're not the right person for the job and finding who is to help you achieve your goal. We'll discuss relationships and networking more later in this book.

Operational Plan

9.   Define a work schedule.

To help you stay on track with your goals and responsibilities, begin by filling in your monthly calendar with notes to mark the dates when you will need to pay for business expenses such as utility bills and re-stocking of supplies. Noting these things on your schedule will help you avoid running out of supplies or encountering late fees on bills and membership dues. By tracking your necessary expenses by date, you can also see how much you need to make from product sales to cover those costs. While this is less important with only one person on the payroll, it becomes infinitely more complex as your business grows. So, it's best to set good practices from the beginning.

Next, come up with a rough schedule for a typical work-week or work-day. In your schedule, include time for all the different necessary responsibilities you will need to do in order to move your business forward. These responsibilities should include time for marketing, creating your products, tracking sales, packaging orders, running to the post office and responding to customer emails. By having a rough idea of what you need to do each day, you eliminate procrastinating when you do not know what to do next and you keep yourself on top of what you need to do to propel your business forward.

Market Research

Though you have already performed some market research to fill in your business plan, additional market research will help you identify your businesses strengths and weaknesses, as well as opportunities for growth or new creative products. But what qualifies as market research? Lots of things, actually, and most are really easy.

Simply logging onto Originl or Etsy and exploring the shops, blogs and portfolios of other artisans and crafters is one easy way to find and observe your competition. You can even research businesses you are not in competition with to determine which of their marketing efforts are effective and which are ineffective. Sometimes looking at a completely different industry can help clearly identifying techniques. As you research other creative businesses, pay close attention to:

- what they are making
- how they are communicating with their fans and followers on social media profiles
- how they describe themselves in blogs and email newsletters
- what their ecommerce shops and websites look like
- how their product descriptions are worded
- how their products are priced
- the quality of their product photos
- and how they are creating demand for their products

Additionally, you can perform market research by asking your friends, family and fans and followers on Facebook and Twitter to offer feedback on everything from your new product ideas to prices, marketing strategies and the colors and template of your business website. This technique is great both to get feedback as well as to engage with the buying community.

7 LEGAL CONSIDERATIONS

When you first start selling your crafts online, you will not need to concern yourself too much with the legal aspects of your business. As your business grows, you will want to consider upgrading to a more fitting business entity and protecting your products with trademarks, patents and copyrights.

Business Entities

Most creative business owners begin conducting business as sole proprietors and establish other business entities as their business needs and liabilities change. Use the following information to compare the tax implications, liability and fees associated with the different types of business entities so that you know which type is best for your business. The good news is, there are options that require little or no upfront effort to establish and have low maintenance.

Sole Proprietorship

A sole proprietorship is a business owned and operated by a single person or a husband and wife team. Because this is a pass-through entity, you will report profits and losses on your personal tax return and you will pay taxes at your individual tax rate.

> **DISCLAIMER**
>
> Legal information found in this book is meant to educate and does not replace professional legal advice. Speak to a lawyer, accountant or small business advisor for assistance in filing business licenses, patents, copyrights and trademarks for your creative business. These professionals can advise you on policies and filing regulations specific to your state or country.

With this business entity, you are personally liable for business debts and legal claims. This means your personal assets can be taken if you are sued or fail to make payments to your debtors. Note that states have different laws regarding which personal assets are subject.

Generally, you don't have to file paperwork or pay any fees to conduct business under this entity. However, many states and cities still require that sole proprietors have a business license in order to conduct business at their location. Visit the Small Business Administration (SBA) website to determine the specific requirements for registering a new business in your state (www.sba.gov/content/incorporating-your-business).

Partnership

A partnership is a business owned and operated by two or more people that are not married. With this pass-through entity, you must file an "informational" tax return each year dividing the profits and losses of the business so that each partner can file their share on their individual tax returns. Each partner is liable for legal claims and business debts. Both partner's assets are subject to legal claims to satisfy a debt, regardless of the partner's stake in the business' profits and losses. Also, any partner can legally bind the entire business to a contract or deal without requiring permission from other partners. As in love, so is in business – it is best to choose your partners wisely!

Forming a partnership is as simple and inexpensive as shaking hands with your potential business partners. However, you may want to hire an accountant to help you prepare a partnership agreement and manage tax returns and documentation for this business entity. You can also seek low cost forms and services from sites such as Legal Zoom (www.legalzoom.com).

Limited Liability Company (LLC)

Similar to a partnership, a business owned and operated by one or more persons that share profits and losses in predetermined proportions is an LLC.

You will file taxes for this business entity on your personal tax returns, just like with partnerships and sole proprietorships. This type of business entity protects the personal assets of all partners, or an individual owner, from most business liabilities. You must file paperwork and pay upfront fees between $500 and $2000 (depending on your state) to become an LLC. You may also have to pay annual fees to retain this business entity.

Given the pass-through nature of filing taxes as well as the legal protections, LLC's are very popular with small businesses. They take a bit more time to establish and maintain than the two options discussed above, but are well worth it if your creative business aspirations are sighted on growth and expansion.

S Corporation

A form of corporation, an S corporation is a business owned by one or more shareholders. An S corporation may have up to 35 shareholders. This entity differs in that while it is a corporation, shareholders do not pay taxes as the corporation. Instead, each shareholder reports the business's profit or loss on their personal income taxes.   S Corporations offer limited liability to protect shareholders from personal loss in relation to the business's debts and financial obligations.   To become an S Corporation, you will need to file and submit Form 2553 with all shareholders information and signatures included when filing your personal taxes. For this reason, filing taxes as an S Corporation is more expensive than filing as an LLC, partnership or sole proprietorship.

Other forms of corporations also exist including C corporations which are not included in this book.   These are typically most appropriate for large business entities with more complex structures. Once your crafty business grows to the size that more elaborate structures are necessary, congratulations, and seek legal counsel.

Although becoming an LLC or S Corporation may protect you from liabilities, those business entities are more expensive to form and require more paperwork. If your creative business will not run many risks or incur many debts, liability insurance will protect you from most legal claims and business debts when operating as a sole proprietorship or partnership. To get liability insurance for your business, speak to a local business insurance agent.

Protecting Your Products and Intellectual Property

You are going to put a lot of work into designing and naming your products and writing up product descriptions, so the last thing you want once you have crafted it perfectly is to find that someone has imitated your unique design or stolen your promotional copy. To prevent a drain on your income and emotions, you may consider the following legal ways to protect your products and intellectual properties.

Copyrights

Copyrights protect written and artistic works from reproduction. While you are protected by U.S. copyright law the moment you create a new work, you will need to register a copyright if you wish to file a lawsuit regarding copyright infringement. You may use copyrights to protect your blog entries, website copy, product descriptions, product photographs and original artworks from theft.

If you have a product that your customers may replicate, such as a pattern for a quilt or outfit, you may protect those products using a creative commons license. This license allows your customers to buy rights to your pattern, so that they can create and sell products using your pattern, but they cannot claim to have created your pattern.

Seek copyright protection for your copy by visiting Copyright Registration on the U.S. Government's Copyright website (www.copyright.gov).

Patents

Because copyright protection does not cover utilitarian crafts such as clothing, jewelry and handbags, you will need a patent to protect those creations from being copied and reproduced by other business entities. To obtain a patent, you will need to file an application with the U.S. Patent and Trademark Office (USPTO), who will then examine your product to determine if it is eligible for protection under either of the two available patent types. The first patent type is a design patent that prevents other people from making and selling products that are substantially similar to the ornamental design of your products. The second patent type, utility patents, prevents others from making products that have functions identical to your product, if your product has a unique function. Due to the famously long periods of time for

U.S. patent applications to be processed, once you file you will be able to use and enjoy the "patent pending" designation.

As of 2011, the U.S. patent process moved to a "first to file" basis. This means that patents are awarded to the first person to successfully file a patent regardless of whether or not they have actually created the item. This is a change from the previous "first to invent" basis which awarded patents to the first to create or invent. So, if you feel your creation is worthy of a patent, it's best to file sooner than later.

You can patent your products yourself by filing an online patent application on the U.S. Patent and Trademark Office's website (www.uspto.gov/patents) and paying a nominal fee. However, you may want to work with a service such as legalzoom.com or an attorney to manage the filing process for you. While this will incur additional fees, it might be worth the peace of mind and free time to focus on your creative projects.

Trademarks

Trademarks protect product names, business names and business symbols from infringement. Trademarks are designated two different symbols: TM and ®; however only ® indicates that the name or symbol has been formally registered with the U.S. Patent and Trademark Office. While you are not required to register formal trademarks for your business or product names, you will need to register if you want to prevent others from using those names for their own business or products. If you have a unique business or product name, a registered trademark is a good idea.

You can file an online trademark application on the U.S. Patent and Trademark Office's website (www.uspto.gov/trademarks) and pay a fee to protect your business and products. As with patents, this is a legal process with defined timelines and review periods, so you may want to work with an attorney or service that specializes in trademark applications. Some services, such as marcaria.com, also file trademark registrations internationally. This might be important if you have a presence in more than the United States.

Take Action!

☑ Speak to a business advisor.

If the process of formally registering your business, obtaining licensing or protecting your property from reproduction intimidates you, then seek out a business advisor to guide you through the process. You can also read books that explain the processes in more detail, go online with services such as legalzoom.com or talk to networking contacts that have knowledge in those areas.

☑ Create a sound foundation for your business.

To find out more about registering and licensing your business, visit the small business administration (SBA) website. To trademark your name or patent your designs, visit the USPTO website.

8 FINANCES AND RECORDKEEPING

As a new business, it is unlikely that you will have the budget to start out with a full staff. In most cases you will be the only employee, serving as both the CEO and water cooler attendant for your business. If this is the case, you will also be in charge of your own recordkeeping activities. This chapter will give you key tips and pointers on keeping track of your finances in order to monitor the progress of your business.

Keeping accurate records is a legal obligation you have to good ol' Uncle Sam, so you might as well start your record-keeping during the planning stages of your business venture. Starting your record-keeping as soon as possible helps you learn to track every expense and sale so that you are not stuck playing catch-up when it becomes vital or without the data you need to make informed decisions.

Begin by gathering all business-related financial documents lying around your house and home office. Store them all together in a file folder or shoe box in your office until you have time to transfer all the details to your business records. Do not wait to transfer your receipts and other important financial documentation to your business records once or twice a year. Instead, plan on updating your files once or twice a month; a little housekeeping once in a while is better than a major meltdown when you are stuck putting in a year's worth of records at one time. Remember, if you leave it all to record at once, you will have no time to accomplish the regular tasks on your growing to-do list. When you're ready to start transferring the details to your business record ledgers, consider scanning all receipts and documents to your computer. This helps to free up storage space in your office and ensures you have a digital copy of all your important papers in case any cash register receipts you have for business expenses fade to white. Plus, by labeling all scanned uploads and filing them into their appropriate folders on your computer, you will have less trouble searching for specific pieces when tax season arrives.

To help keep your business expenses and profits separate from your personal financials, open a separate banking account for your business. In most cases you will need only a $50 or $100 deposit to start this new account. As an added bonus, many banks provide online banking features that allow you to categorize your business expenses and generate helpful reports you can use to make necessary adjustments on your spending.

If you will be financing your business expenses with a credit card, use a separate credit card account to keep personal and business expenses and finances separate so you can avoid later frustrations and confusion. Centralizing business purchases with a credit card can also simplify or eliminate cash receipt recording, not to mention the potential of reward or airline points which can help you take that much needed vacation to treat yourself.

Consider taking a basic accounting class from your local community college or state university to learn the basic record-keeping processes and forms you will need for your creative business. You may also be able to take those courses and seek counseling from your local Small Business Development Center (SMDC), where you can ask to have your education tailored to your art or craft industry business.

The good news is you don't need to start from scratch and record everything on blank paper. If you do your recordkeeping this way, as your business grows you'll spend all your time keeping records updated. Use computer programs and online services to quickly track records that you can easily search as necessary. Programs and services available for a free or paid membership include Quicken (quicken.intuit.com), FreshBooks (www.freshbooks.com), Outright (www.outright.com) and Quick Books (quickbooks.intuit.com). Bear in mind that available features vary according to membership levels. However, you may also use Microsoft Excel (office.microsoft.com/en-us/excel) or EverNote (www.evernote.com), the former of which is standard on most PC computers while the latter is available for free download to any computer operating system.

What records should you keep?

Until you can invest in a class or book to learn more about basic accounting, we are going to discuss the types of records you should be keeping to make the process of filing and paying your taxes a little less intimidating.

Purchases

You should be keeping track of any purchases you make of items that you resell to your customers. This includes purchases of art or crafting supplies and materials you use to make your creative products. To track your purchases, save your check stubs, invoices and credit card and cash register sales receipts and record these in your tracking program or spreadsheet by product type.

Expenses

Expenses are costs you incur operating your business. Expenses vary from purchases and include such things as utility bills, rent payments and membership dues. Collect and file all receipts, invoices, petty cash slips and bank account statements documenting payment of your expenses.

You may also incur business expenses related to transportation, travel and entertainment. These expenses often arise when you are treating potential clients to a meeting over lunch or travelling across the nation to attend a major arts fair or gift show to showcase your creations. In these cases, you may need to prove that the expense is business-related. If you traveled to attend an arts and craft fair, keep documentation of airline receipts as well as any brochures you can pick up at the event. If you are showcasing your work, keep documentation that shows you paid your booth fees, as well as any brochures, flyers or business cards you gave away at the event.

Assets

The term "assets" describes any property that you own and use at your place of business. Assets may include machinery you use to manufacture your creative products or furniture and devices that you use when conducting business, such as your computer, desk and swivel chair. Documentation that you should collect and file in regards to your assets include receipts detailing when and how they were acquired, repair costs and invoices, invoices for upgrades to assets, details regarding how the asset was used and how the asset was donated or disposed of. You should also keep track of the depreciation of your assets so that you can take deductions on your tax return for the depreciation amount.

Inventory

Your creative products that are finished and ready for sale are your inventory. Keeping track of your inventory is pretty straight-forward. Start a spreadsheet to monitor the movement of your inventory. In your spreadsheet, you can keep track of product descriptions, prices and attach photos, so that your product information is all in one place when you are uploading that info to different ecommerce sites. Add a column on your spreadsheet to mark when each item sells, so that you can examine the sheet later to see which products sell best, in what colors and variations. This can help you prepare stock and alter your product focus. Several online sites where you can sell your creations also allow you to enter inventory of the same or similar items so you do not oversell and under-deliver.

Gross Receipts

Collect and file invoices, PayPal statements, bank statements, bank deposit slips, credit card slips and receipt books that document income you receive from your business and creative products. This helps you track your topline revenue as well as which products sell during specific months or seasons. With this, forecast future sales and plan for busy seasons by pre-stocking the most popular items.

At Originl, we help simplify the process of record-keeping by offering features to track your sales and product inventory. As an added bonus, using Originl's features, you can track the popularity of each product by both sales numbers and by which items receive the most views. Using this information, you can drop low-profit products and observe what your customers love most, so that you can plan future products to appeal to your existing customer-base.

Paying Taxes

Whether you plan on outsourcing your tax filing to an accountant, or you intend on tackling it yourself, there are a few things you should know to help you maximize your deductions and get the most from your tax return.

First of all, did you know that you can get a tax deduction for running your business out of your home? You sure can. Actually, you can write off deductions for the percentage of your home used as your business. However, you need to be careful if you plan on writing off a portion of your home to get deductions for your office space; if you ever decide to move, some states require that you pay back any deducted amounts before you can sell your home.

If you file your own taxes, you will probably be tempted to whip through them quickly; however, to get the tax return you deserve, you will want to consider itemizing. Itemizing means that you will need to list assets, expenses and purchases related to your business on the appropriate tax forms, so that you can receive the deductions you are entitled to. Knowing exactly how to itemize, what to itemize and what you can get deductions for may not be in your skill set, in which case, it's not too expensive to outsource to an accountant. You can also use online tax filing programs and services such as Turbo Tax (www.turbotax.com) and Tax Act (www.taxact.com). With these, when you are ready to file you can pay an extra protection fee to protect yourself against an audit.

Another thing to consider is to pay your taxes quarterly instead of waiting until the end of the year to pay the taxes you owe at one time. When you pay quarterly, you will need to reference your sales and income records so that you can estimate how much you owe quarterly. Don't worry, you don't have to get your quarterly payments exactly right. If you overpay you'll get it back on your tax return and if you underpay, you can make up the difference when filing your taxes.

These are some basic tax tips to get you started; however, the tax law can be quite complex. So, consider consulting an accountant for further advice and assistance with deductions, itemizing, and payment options.

Sales Tax

A common question most new businesses have, especially when selling online, is if they are required to pay sales tax. This is a variable answer and first depends on what state your business is based in. This is the state you live in (your headquarters) or have a branch store. If this state collects sales tax, you need to acquire a permit and pay sales tax. The best place to start looking is your state government's website.

Go to the taxation section and look for details on obtaining a sales tax permit as well as how to file and pay sales tax.

Even if you are selling completely online, you will still need to abide by sales tax laws. If you sell to someone who lives in the same state, even if that sale is made online, you are required to collect and pay sales tax. If you sell to someone in a different state, then there's no need to charge sales tax. Hurray! Most websites take care of this for you by automatically calculating appropriate sales tax for you.

After you receive your sales tax permit, you simply need to file and pay sales tax with your state each year in addition to income tax as appropriate for your business entity. If you have a physical store or sell at craft fairs, it's also typically required to display your sales tax permit.

Take Action!

☑   Learn more about basic accounting and record-keeping.

Read a book or take a basic accounting class to learn about the different financial statements you will need to organize in order to keep track of your business spending and income. The Accounting Game, by Darrel Mullis and Judith Orloff (www.amazon.com/Accounting-Game-Basic-Fresh-Lemonade/dp/1402211864), is an easy-to-follow guide through the world of accounting. You can also learn a lot by visiting the recordkeeping resources on the Small Business Administration's (SBA) website.

☑   Get your affairs in order.

Spend a day creating spreadsheets on your computer to keep records of your business expenses and revenue. Add in information about your initial purchases and inventory for your business. By taking the time to set all of this up before you make your first sale, you will avoid the frustration of organizing it all later, when you are busy making sales and filling orders.

9 PRICING YOUR CREATIONS

Now that you are starting to get a basic idea of all that you will want to do to keep your creative business running, you will need to make sure you are pricing your products correctly – high enough to pay yourself for your time and keep your business profitable. This is an area where a lot of people get their business in trouble. Instead of pricing with profit in mind, they price emotionally based on what they think is a fair price for their products. Sure, you may think your fair prices will attract more customers, but if you are undercharging, your low compensation will distract you from enjoying your work and this will quickly send your business into the red.

This chapter will review the key factors to consider and take a simple formulaic approach to pricing your creations.

Business Overhead

In the language of business, overhead refers to the ongoing operating expenses of your business. Your business's overhead includes the following expenses and more necessary to keep your business's virtual doors open:

- Rent
- Electricity
- Advertising
- Accounting fees
- Telephone bills
- Internet service
- Legal fees
- Membership fees
  (for services you use to sell your products, keep records or manage your social media profiles; business associations you are part of; and even for membership with your local chamber of commerce)
- Travel expenses
- Shipping costs
- PayPal processing fees
- Credit card processing fees
- Marketing costs
- Business equipment maintenance and supplies
  (printer ink is just one example)
- Insurance rates

Do the math to figure out how much your overhead is per month, then divide that value by the approximate number of hours your business is open (the hours you are working) each month. This will give you an estimate of how much you are spending per hour on your business. This is your overhead cost that serves as the baseline above which you will price your products. Of course, the lower you can keep your overhead costs, the higher your profit margins can be not to mention lower stress of paying those fixed expenses.

Cost of Supplies

Technically, supplies are considered part of the overhead cost of running your business. However, let's set this factor of pricing out of overhead given the nature of your business. Instead, you should derive an estimated cost of supplies for each product that you make. For example, you may spend $250 a month on jewelry supplies, but each piece that you make uses a different type or amount of hardware. When painting on an extra-large gallery wrapped canvas, your costs are higher than on sketch paper. If you look at it this way, how much you spend on supplies per month is irrelevant; instead, it's important to know how much you spend on supplies for each product you make.

Expand your financial tracking spreadsheet to include costs and units of supplies required per product. Track this over time to get an accurate measure.

The Value of Your Time

Finally, when deciding on a price for your creations, you need to figure out how much you want to make as your hourly wage and how long it takes you to make each product. This includes the time you spend actually creating the product and more. You also need to consider the time you spend photographing, writing product descriptions, packaging orders and time spent taking care of regular shipping issues. You should consider time spent prototyping or trying out new techniques. You might even consider all the hours you spend working on anything related to your business, such as blogging, marketing and updating your business records. If you do not know what you want to give yourself as an hourly wage, look at how many hours per week you spend working and then look at how much money you will need to make to cover your personal bills, in addition to your business expenses. Be reasonable, but set this high enough to be satisfied or match your financial goals.

Now, add the hourly wage you have in mind to the hourly overhead of your business and the supply cost for each creative product you make. (You should have a different price for each piece, if the creation time and supply costs vary between each product.) And, there you have it – your product prices!

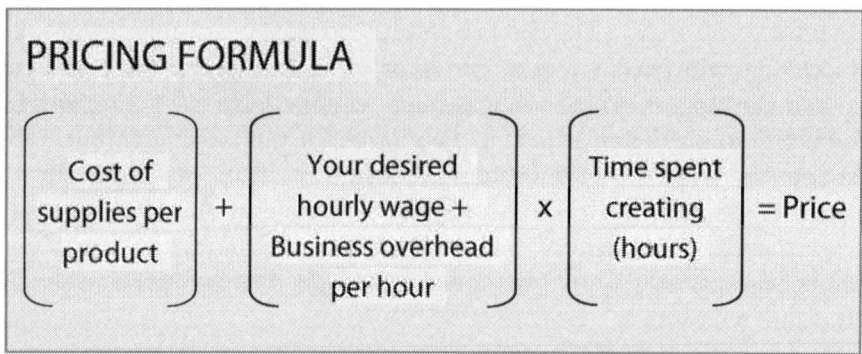

With your prices in mind, it is time to do some market research to see how your prices compare to your competition and to see if potential customers are receptive to your prices.

Begin by looking online to see what other artisans are charging for similar pieces. Do your prices seem fair in comparison to others you are in competition with or those putting their own creative spin on products similar to your own? Don't pay attention to the cost of similar, mass-merchandised items; your pieces are unique and handmade. You have a right to price them higher than mass-produced items. In fact, higher prices may help differentiate you from mass manufactured comparables.

Next, ask your friends and family to tell you what they think about the prices you have in mind for each of your products. Do they think your prices are fair? Remind them that your products are handmade and offer a special uniqueness that you cannot get from mass-produced items.

Alter your prices, as necessary, using your market research results and feedback. However, be careful you to not lower your prices so low that you cannot pay yourself a reasonable wage or cover your business overhead; that's the guaranteed quickest way to lose interest in your business and fail to turn a profit.

Your original prices may require altering throughout the life of your business. Using your sales data as well as popularity of items, increase or decrease prices and observe how that impacts sales. Using features built into the Originl community site, if a creation is viewed often but sales are low, consider reducing your price to meet the budget of your buyers. Just make sure you are not stooping below a price you are willing to accept. If it is viewed often and sales are high often resulting in selling out, consider increasing your price to match the demand.

Pricing Psychology

You may have seen prices and wondered if charging a few cents more or less really makes a difference. Interestingly, the format of your pricing can influence your buyers. So before you slap your prices onto your products in an online shop or at a local retail location, we will discuss a few key points of pricing psychology. The psychology of pricing explains how retailers use the numbers in a product's price to signal to buyers that the product is high-quality or offered at the lowest price possible. Take a look at the different types of price endings and what those prices communicate to consumers.

Prices That End In .99

Why should you charge $24.99 for your handmade goldfish-shaped earrings, instead of $25.00? Because consumers tend to pay attention only to the numbers on the left side of the decimal point in a product's price. So, instead of noticing that your product costs a penny short of $25, customers will see those first two digits and think your product costs 99 cents less than it actually does. These are cues to the buyer that it is less expensive than the actual price. This is especially important at certain threshold prices such as $1, $5, $10, $100 which are psychologically significant and different for different products. For example, an e-book for $0.99 sounds like an amazing deal over $1. A flat screen TV for $499.99 is a value over $500. Typically prices that end in .95 are not treated differently than .99, so you might as well price it higher and receive the extra 4 cents.

Prices With More Precise Endings

Most prices you see when you're shopping in-store or online end with .99 or .00. However, you may have noticed that a few retailers end their product prices with an unusual cent value, such as $4.74, $29.97, $54.73. These precise price endings send the signal to customers that a product is being offered at the lowest price the producer or seller can afford to offer the customer and still turn a profit.

Prices Without Cent Value

Prices that do not contain a cent value - $35.00, $175.00, $300.00 – convey the message that a product is of premium quality. This pricing method is the standard for high-end and luxury brands and is a great method to use to distinguish that your creative products have a special quality that you cannot get when buying similar products from mass merchandisers.

Sales & Discounts

Offering sales and discounts on your products may be an effective way to increase your product sales and attract more customers. However, to maintain your creations as unique higher end products, you need to be careful about how you offer those sales and discounts. If you grow into the habit of hosting seasonal sales, your customers may wait to buy from you when they know you're going to put items on sale. Similarly, if you are offering sales and discounts too often, you might as well lower your regular prices because offering sales too often tells your customers that your products are not really worth the original prices you listed.

To ensure you do not devalue your time and your creative products, consider the following recommendations for offering sales and discounts.

One-Day Sales

It can be effective to offer seasonal sales, but if too many customers start waiting on your sales, your profit margin will suffer. To ensure you don't lose money by offering sales, try offering seasonal sales for one day only. If you sell a lot of products prior to Christmas, try offering a one day sale on Black Friday or Cyber Monday. Similarly, you can offer one-day sales on other special days throughout the year, such as the anniversary of when you first opened your online shop. You can even choose sale days that relate to your product line or shop name. Because their jewelry charms include several inedible, miniature pies, Jessica and Susan Partain of Inedible Jewelry offer a special sale every year on March 14, Pi Day. How fun is that!

Discounts for Repeat Customers

Let your customers know that you appreciate their business and encourage them to become repeat customers by offering discounts on future purchases they make. To do this, simply include a coupon code when shipping orders out to your customers.

Special Discounts

Think a specific group of people within your target market deserve a discount on your products? Give it to them. Advertise the discount by mentioning it on your website, shop bio and blog. Alexandra Koiv at Alex in Welderland's Custom Pet Urns offers a 15% discount to customers purchasing pet urns for service dogs. This type of discount is not necessarily to increase sales, but can definitely help you build customer admiration for your business ethic and mission.

Trade Favors for Discounts

Need a promotional service, some copy written for your website or some free crafting supplies? Trade product discounts with artists and other professionals who can help you with supplies or services you need for your business. Lauren Kilbourne, owner of The Littlest Feather, offers a 10% discount to customers that send her an appreciation photo of themselves wearing her jewelry. In turn, she replaces existing product images on her shop with the customer appreciation photos, because she feels modeled photos of her jewelry give customers a better idea of how her pieces look when worn.

Sales to Move Products

If you want to move inventory that is taking too much room in your studio (and your mind), then perhaps you should consider a special sale. You can avoid devaluing your time and sending the wrong signal to your customers by offering sales and discounts on only a few products at a time. Additionally, you can advertise end-of-year sales or closeout sales to move excess inventory on numerous products for a short period of time. To move excess products, you may offer over-stocked items on BOGO (buy one get one free) or B2G1F (buy two get one free) sales.

Discounts for Your Slow Seasons

Have a few weeks or months every year that your sales slow down? Try offering special discounts during those seasons so that the down time does not cause you to lose money. Laura Kelly, owner of peaceloveglass, combats her autumn slow season by offering customers free shipping and a small product discount if they place their Christmas orders during the first week of her slow sales season.

Discounts for Large Orders

If you want to encourage customer to place bulk orders or thank customers for placing large orders, offer a discount. Set the discount amount as desired and specify for your own record how many pieces your customers must order to receive the discount. You don't have to advertise this type of discount, but your customers will appreciate a discount when they order in bulk and that appreciation will lead them to remember you the next time they need to order numerous pieces at one time.

Social media channels are also good uses for product promotions. Experiment with giving away a few of your creative products or coupons on your social media profiles and to the readers of blogs whose audience also fall within your target market. You could even give away your products to friends and family members to use or as gifts or party favors to give your business and products some free promotion and word-of-mouth advertising. The options are endless. Get creative!

TIP

Here are a few ways to offer coupon discounts:

Send coupon codes with each product you sell to encourage repeat customers.

Share a coupon code with your followers on your social media profiles.

Hand out coupons at in-person sales events such as craft fairs.

Experiment with daily deal sites like LivingSocial.com and Groupon.com.

10 SELLING ONLINE

You now have a name for your creative business, defined your product and brand and have a business plan. You understand your expenses, have developed a pricing strategy and have an inventory of finished creations ready to sell.

Let's open up shop!

A decade ago, if you wanted to sell your arts and crafts, you would probably focus your efforts on local customers, selling primarily at art and craft fairs and offering your products for sale in shops on consignment. Even in the late 1990s and early 2000s, when Internet business was taking deep root, charting an online course for your business might have left you in troubled waters. You could have created a simple website or shopping cart. However, you would probably have had trouble setting up a shop that tailored to your unique products and would have had to deal with the time-consuming process of generating traffic to your site. If you build it, they don't always come.

Fortunately, over more recent years, Internet business and ecommerce has evolved. You now have many different online venues to choose from when it comes to selling your artwork and crafts online. Artisans and crafters are no longer limited to opening up a single brick-and-mortar business, working with galleries or selling only to a local market. Modern day creatives can open a handful of different shops online to reach a larger audience of consumers and ultimately sell more of their handmade creations.

While there are a variety of online selling venues for you to choose from, let's focus your efforts on some of the most popular ones that are more uniquely suited to your business.

Your Own Store

A more traditional model to ecommerce is creating your own website. If you are set on selling your products through your own website e-store, consider services which make this process much easier than building from scratch. Services such as Shopify (www.shopify.com), Big Cartel (www.bigcartel.com) and Big Commerce (www.bigcommerce.com) offer the ability to design and customize shops, and even purchase domains and hosting or hook their shops to existing websites.

> ## SNEAK PEEK
>
> In the chapters ahead, we will discuss marketing and promotion strategies to drive potential customers to your online shop.

Each of these ecommerce services offer different membership levels that vary in price and features. While only Big Cartel currently offers a free membership level, both Shopify and Big Commerce offer free trials so you can give each service a test drive and find one you are comfortable with before upgrading to a plan that fits your needs. With monthly memberships between $9.99 and $299.95, these options are the more expensive choices.

Consider these as your business grows and you are looking for a standalone presence or more features. This model works best once you have an established marketing channel, traffic and existing customers. Otherwise, you may be left with a sharp looking e-store, but no sales.

Online Auctions

Online auction sites like eBay (www.ebay.com), Webstore (www.webstore.com), and Online Auction (www.onlineauction.com) offer a lower-cost entry level option for selling your crafts online and providing an existing source of traffic and potential buyers. At eBay you can list up to 50 products per month for free; but once you make a sale, eBay will deduct 9% of your total product price (including shipping, handling and any additional charges) as a service fee. A more budget-friendly but less popular option may be Online Auction, where you can list as many products as you want for a fixed-price membership of only $8 per month. And thanks to their advertising sponsors, Webstore allows their sellers to keep 100% of their profits – this means there are no listing fees, membership fees or commissions deducted from your revenue.

Despite their budget-friendly prices and existing traffic, online auction sites are crowded markets with such diverse products that consumers may have trouble finding your creations. If your handmade creations and artistic masterpieces are listed next to reproductions or mass-produced items at a fraction of the cost, your sales will suffer and your brand may be tarnished. Listing on sites that specialize in artwork and handmade crafts may be a better option.

Online Marketplaces

Several online marketplaces exist that focus specifically on the sale of handmade art and crafts. These include some highly trafficked sites like Etsy (www.etsy.com), Artfire (www.artfire.com), Dawanda (www.dawanda.com), Zibbet (www.zibbet.com) and our own Originl (www.originl.com). Because these sites offer primarily handmade products, many artisans and crafters find these websites the most successful online venues for selling creative products. These sites are usually easy to set up and charge easy-to-afford listing and sales fees.

Etsy – perhaps the most popular online marketplace for creatives – allows you to post as many products as you want, for a list price of 20 cents per item; when you make a sell, you will pay 3.5% of the product price (not including shipping) as a transaction fee for using Etsy's service. At Artfire, you will pay a flat rate membership of $11.95 per month with no listing or transaction fees, plus your first month is on the house. You can list items for free at Dawanda and pay a 5% commission to the site for every sale processed through their service. And at Zibbet, you can choose from a free, basic membership or a premium membership that costs only $9.95; with both memberships you will pay no listing or commission fees, but with the free membership you are limited to listing only 50 total items.

This class of niche online marketplace site is a great choice for selling online. If you have not tried one or more of them, give them a try. Many creative find listing in multiple sites effective. However, though these venues are affordable, they rarely offer any features beyond the ability to post pictures and descriptions of items for sale and process payments. To expand beyond this, you may want to create a standalone website or blog and link to your online marketplace store.

Originl

Our own Originl creative community marketplace (www.originl.com) is also an online selling platform designed especially for artists and crafters. However, we like to think that we stand out from the others. In addition to offering you a place to list items, Originl also offers unique social features to help you brand your business, interact with your potential buyers and build relationships with and draw inspiration from a community of other creative entrepreneurs.

It's easy to get started at Originl, and you can sell your creative products a low fixed cost, depending on your membership level. What's more, we play well with others! You can use Originl to promote your business and link to your products for sale on Etsy or other marketplace sites. You will be most successful with a blended strategy of online selling and branding. We will discuss this more later on.

Online Classifieds

Some crafters even find online classifieds websites such as Craigslist (www.craigslist.com) and Classifieds for Free (www.classifiedsforfree.com) effective at generating sales and growing your customer-base. Sales are not directly processed through these locations; instead, these venues serve as a place to post ads for your sites. Post photos and descriptions of your products in your free ads and leave contact information readers can use to find your online shop, connect with you on social media, visit your website or send you an email to place an order. This is another tool you can consider as part of your blended strategy.

Take Action!

☑   Find your spot.

Explore the different online venues mentioned and decide on which places you want to use to sell your creative products. You may want to start out in only one and then expand. A good recommendation is to start selling your products in at least two different places, then you can add or drop different venues as you see how successful you are in each virtual location. Consider site features, cost, and the availability of existing traffic of potential buyers. Leveraging sites that accomplish more than just selling can help you build your business and keep overhead costs lower.

11 ONLINE SELLING TIPS

Listing your products for sale online is an important step, but doesn't guarantee revenue for your creative venture. In the following chapters, we will cover techniques to make your business a success. Before we jump into a discussion about marketing and promoting your business, we need to make sure that you create a great virtual shop that converts visitors into fans and customers.

Photographing Your Creations

When it comes to selling your creations online, that old adage about the value of a photograph could not be more accurate. Good product pictures equal more sales. Different from selling in a physical store, visitors to online stores cannot pick up and inspect the quality of your creations. Product photos are key to conveying the size, color, construction and uniqueness of your projects. Product photos can often make the difference in a great product that sells or does not.

Here are a few key tips for making your product photos the best they can be.

- Use a quality camera to take great photos. If you do not have one of your own, borrow one or hire a local photographer until you can invest in one. Even fairly inexpensive compact digital cameras can take great photos, and they are worth the investment.

- Study your camera's user manual to learn more about light settings, exposure and other photography basics that will help you get the most perfect pictures of your products. Simply adjusting the light settings to match your environment (tungsten, fluorescent, daylight) can make a dramatic difference in the resulting photographs.

- Invest in a tripod for your camera and a light diffuser to steady your camera and take exceptional, well-lit photos that show off the details of your creative products. Inexpensive photography kits are available online from Amazon.com and other sites that typically include lights, diffusers and a tripod. These are a good idea to consider.

- Stage product photos using a simple background of white or another solid color. Avoid taking photos of products with a busy backdrop that will clash with and distract attention from your products. Also, if staging photos using the backdrop of your living room, desk or studio, clean up any clutter and strewn craft supplies to prevent distracting potential customers.

- Edit your photos, as necessary, using free programs like Picnik (www.picnik.com) and Picasa (picasa.google.com) on your computer to remove red-eye from models and glare in your product pictures. Try different photo editing tools to find the one that you are most comfortable using.

- Take multiple photos of each product so your customers get a clear view of what they are buying. This will make them less hesitant to buy your products. Snap shots of your pieces from different angles and, if your product is wearable, take modeled photos of your product, to give your customers an idea of what your pieces look like when wore. Additionally, take close-up photographs of your creative products to showcase the intricate details on both small and large items.

Demonstrational Videos

If you have a functional product that cannot be demonstrated well-enough with still photographs then consider creating a video that will give your shoppers a more in-depth look at your products. To do this, you will need a video camera and basic video editing program for your computer, tablet or smart phone. You will also want to use studio lighting to make high-quality videos that enhance your product listing, not detract from it. This is easier than it may seem, so give it a shot and stand out from the crowd.

Once your videos are shot and edited, you can upload them to YouTube (www.youtube.com), Vimeo (www.vimeo.com) or another video hosting website. Then, add a link to your demonstrational videos at the end of your product descriptions. Additionally, you can create an entire channel on any video hosting website to demonstrate and promote your products at low or no cost. Be sure to include references to your website or e-store address.

Crafting Effective Product Descriptions

A good product description paints a picture in your shoppers' minds and can help turn browsers into buyers. Unfortunately, finding a balance between sounding like a pushy car salesperson and showing your passion for your work can leave you at a loss for words.

Combat your writer's block by researching your competition. If you don't know the first thing about writing product descriptions, the most logical thing to do is find some and read them. Carefully read through the product description prose in the shops of other artisans and crafters, those offering products similar to or different from your own. As you read, notice the difference between the product descriptions that appeal to you and those that are just average. Pay special attention to the wording, voice and imagery in the product descriptions that really draw you in.

Then, do a little brainstorming and write down key points that you want, and need, to mention about your product. As you do this, pretend that your customers will not be able to look at photos of your products; pretend that they must rely solely on how you describe your products in words. After all, your photos cannot portray the emotion, thought and passion of your pieces like a well written description does.

As you jot down notes about what to include in your descriptions, remember the following key details that your customers may want to know when looking at and buying your products:

- Dimensions
- Materials
- Colors
- Techniques used in creation
- Care and maintenance
- Who is the product for
- What is its function
- Texture
- Why is it unique
- When can you use it
- Where can you display it

With all this in mind, create another list of those key points, listing the most important information first; this is the information you will want to write into the first few sentences of your product description.

As you write each product description, you may want to begin with a fun story about your product or a visual depiction before you list those other product details that are better suited for the end of your product descriptions. As a guide, shoot for a word count between 75 and 200 words to accurately and thoroughly describe your products, specify their use and explain why your products are different from your competition. At the end of product descriptions, you can include links to demonstrational videos, other products in the same collection or matching accessories also available in your shop.

Keep in mind your overall business brand and strategy. After writing a description, ask yourself if it is true to your brand and how you want to be portrayed. Do your descriptions relate to your vision and mission as a designer? Do they tie in to your brand image? Consistency is important in all public messaging you push out, including product descriptions and will help you stand out from the competition.

Following are a few samples of real, effective product descriptions from other creative shop owners. Use these not as templates, but as inspirations for your own unique product descriptions.

Pumpkin Pie necklace from Inedible Jewelry

A delicious little inedible pumpkin pie for your neck! This handmade necklace is the perfect accessory (or hostess gift!) for Thanksgiving.

We sculpted the tiny pie by hand from polymer clay. The pie is in a tiny, shiny pie plate, the crust has little hand-pinched indentations, the pie filling is perfectly spiced, and the whipped cream looks like it's fresh from the can. The necklace is beaded by hand with tiny sparkly copper-lined Japanese seed beads. It's strung on braided steel wire for strength and security, and finished with a silver-plated lobster clasp.

Measurements: The pumpkin pie measures just over 3/4" (2cm) in diameter. The necklace is 16" long; see the fourth photo for a sense of scale. If you'd prefer a longer necklace, contact us and we'll be happy to make you a custom one.

Gift boxed: All of our pieces come ready for gift-giving in a happy white box tied with colorful ribbon.

Click here for matching pumpkin pie dangly earrings.

Click here for pumpkin pie stud earrings.

Prefer cherry pie earrings? Maybe you're more of a cherry pie person? No problem!

Check out the rest of our shop: http://inediblejewelry.etsy.com

Contact us to request your custom treat!

Please see our shop policies page for our complete store policies, shipping and payment information, and FAQ.

Thanks for stopping in!
Jessica & Susan

Some crafters find it useful to come up with quirky names for products or group them into funky collections to help inspire the copy for descriptions. This can help relay your personality and that of your brand to potential buyers. Your customers are interested in buying your creations not just because they are unique but also because they are buying, well, you! Don't be afraid to let them know your personality, even in your product descriptions.

Following is an example of such an approach for Ollie, the owl finger puppet pictured below.

Ollie the Owl Finger Puppet by Stacey Rebecca Gordon

Ollie the Owl finger puppet glides through the night air swiftly & quietly, looking for munchies.

Ollie the Owl finger puppet is a part of the Food Chain Friends collection, a series of finger puppets that have puppet pals that they can either eat, or that will eat them (sold separately). Ollie's Food Chain Friends: Owl eats mouse. Mouse eats corn. Corn eats butter. Butter eats heart.

Ollie the Owl is made of 100% wool felt. The natural lanolin in the wool makes it soft and smooth. And sheep are a 100% renewable resource! Add that up & it's like 200% awesome. Ollie the Owl comes with his own wooden puppet stand & inside of a clear, plastic, cylindrical box for all of your collectible, dust-free, gift-giving, display-loving needs.

Ollie the Owl is quite versatile & perfect for work desks and shelves, as well as table top puppet theaters, sitting in church pews, rides in a car or airplane, grandma's purse, playroom baskets, trips to the grocery store, and fancy restaurants.

Puppets help kids build language and social skills in an imaginative, fun way. They facilitate healthy communication for all age groups, giving kids and adults an emotionally safe way to express themselves. They enhance story time, classroom learning, and are overall just plain fun to have around.

Ollie the Owl may look quite delicious; however, he's only safe for children ages 3 and up.

Want to bring Ollie, Miles, Caroline, Beatrice, and Harry home with you? Buy all 5 and save $8.00!

http://puppetpie.blogspot.com
http://www.puppetpie.com

12 MARKETING – CREATING DEMAND

You know you make amazing things. Now let's make sure potential buyers know it.

Marketing efforts are a key part of communicating to your potential customers about your products so you generate enough sales to keep your dream creative business thriving. Marketing gets your product out there, in the public eye, so that you get more traffic to your online shop and ultimately make more sales.

Marketing is a broad topic that includes many business activities, but simply stated, the term marketing refers to activities you do to promote your business and create demand with potential customers to purchase your products. Some of the techniques you have already learned to do in this book are forms of marketing. Offering sales is a form of marketing; everyone loves a bargain, and they love to tell their friends about it too. That means information about your products and company is reaching more people. Product descriptions also count as a form of marketing; good descriptions deliver all the details your shoppers want to know about your product but may not think to ask.

But marketing extends beyond those topics we have already covered in this book and includes such practices as building relationships with customers, online and offline product promotion, engaging is social media and advertising. Even optimizing your shop, product descriptions, website copy and business blog posts with keywords to generate better search engine results falls under the umbrella of marketing.

Because marketing includes so many different techniques, it is often confused with selling because the two terms – marketing and selling – are often misused interchangeably. This is typically because marketing and selling can overlap and involve similar activities. For example, networking and responding to inquiries from customers are actions that straddle the fence between marketing and selling, as you can use those practices both to promote your product and close sales. However, despite the occasional overlap there is a distinct difference between marketing and selling. It is important to understand this distinction to gauge the effectiveness of both concepts and make improvements where necessary.

An easy way to understand the difference is to remember that marketing is what you do to prepare for a sale, while selling is the process of closing the sale. When you are marketing, you are creating a demand for your product, finding customers interested in your product and delivering them all the information they need to know to find your shop and buy your products. When you are in the selling process, you are working one-on-one with each customer, even if it is virtually, to make their experience with you one they find irresistible and will remember. This is key for after sale passive marketing such as word-of-mouth promotion of your products to their friends.

In the following chapters, we are going to shift focus and start to discuss the many different ways to market. Before we do, you need to know a few basics about how to market and the most effective strategies for your creative business.

To ensure your marketing measures convert to sales, you must convince consumers that they actually need – must have – your product. In the business world, this is known as creating demand. This can be difficult, especially for a creative product that buyers may not *actually* need. Luckily, handmade products are generally in demand. In recent years, there has been a movement – called the handmade movement – rejecting mass-produced goods and encouraging the sale of handcrafted treasures. After all, who wants something everyone else has when they can own something truly unique? We all love a good conversation piece!

Even though handmade items are already in demand, it is a big world out there. There are a lot of artists and crafters with the same entrepreneurial dream and many likely working in your same medium. You still have to create demand for your own specific product and let consumers know what sets you apart from the other artists in your medium. In design, remember this is sometimes known as your "zebra". What is unique or different about you? What sets you apart from the rest of the herd?

One way to create demand is to let your personality and passion for your products show in your marketing efforts. It's not quite as easy as proclaiming, "I love my products and you will too." Consumers already know you love what you do; now you have to let your passion show in how you craft your marketing messages. This can cause others to get enthusiastic about your products too.

You create demand with passionate prose in product descriptions, blog posts and status updates on your business' social media profiles. In addition, you can get consumers passionate about your product by writing text that lets them know why your product is just what they need to add a finishing touch to their living room, satisfy that hard-to-shop-for gift or encourage their imagination.

Further complement your marketing measures by creating a portfolio to showcase your work. While the lineup in your online shop will serve as a makeshift showcase of your products, most shops are limited to listing what you have in stock and only the products available for sale. By creating a portfolio, you have freedom to showcase past work, test new products, get feedback from consumers and give customers more products to choose from. You can add a portfolio to your business website or easily create one using our own Originl community site.

Remember also back to our discussion of creating your business plan and knowing your target audience.   None of your marketing efforts will ever return profit for your time and money if you don't remember to tailor your marketing messages and measures to fit your target market of potential buyers. Always keep your audience in mind as you market, and you will quickly build a strong following and ultimately sell more of your products.

Take Action!

☑ **Define your business personality.**

Create a list of adjectives that describe your business personality. Refer to these when creating your marketing messaging to ensure your voice is consistent and portrays your brand personality.

☑ **Create a portfolio.**

Gather together your favorite or most popular creations that showcase your creative business and illustrate your product range. Build an online portfolio with product photos and descriptions as part of your e-store or separate to showcase your brand.

13 BE FOUND ONLINE

Marketing is an incredibly important task, but can sometimes feel like a time-consuming effort, especially in the beginning of your business adventure. And, let's face it, you would rather be in your workshop, slinging paint, beading, welding, stitching or whatever it is you do. Instead of looking for potential customers, let's make it easier for your potential customers to find you.

You can help yourself and your future fans by making yourself easier to find online. By launching a web presence, starting a blog and learning the art of search engine optimization, you and your products will be easier to find by those who are looking. While this will not replace marketing efforts (which we will talk about further in later chapters), you can create a passive source of traffic freeing up much valued time to create more amazing creations to sell in your shop.

Create a Website

Not every crafter finds it relevant to launch a website early on in addition to having a shop on Originl, Etsy or other marketplaces. However, creating a website and blog is a super way to passively market your business, especially if you are optimizing your site with keywords your potential customers may use to find your products. Having a website in companion to your shop is a great way to make your business look professional and gives your business a web address you can include in online and offline promotional pieces. This will help your customers and connections find you online.

Don't worry; you do not have to be a web design genius to create a website these days – though hiring a web or graphic design freelancer is certainly an option. Web design services like WordPress (www.wordpress.com), SquareSpace (www.squarespace.com) and Weebly (www.weebly.com) make it so easy to create a website that your mother could probably figure it out. These sites are full service including hosting and allow you to buy your own domain name. This means you can take their names out of your website's url address and have a simple, clean dot-com all your own. You can also integrate a shop or link to your shop at Originl or Etsy and host a blog all on the same website.

I suggest researching WordPress, SquareSpace, Weebly and a handful of other website building services to find the site that best fits your web design experience and offers templates that follow the theme of your business and products. These services typically offer templates or themes which alter the look and feel of the site. You can purchase additional themes, make your own or have a theme created for you, though the last two options may require that you hire a web designer or trade favors with a friend that is familiar with HTML.

Once you find a service to use to build your website, it's time to choose a domain name. As you navigate this process, keep in mind any changes and updates you want to make to your website in the future. Also, do you plan on using a separate email address for your business, or do you want your email address to include your domain name, such as "something@youdomain.com"? This is a nice touch and makes your business look more professional than a Gmail or an ol' AOL email address. Both Weebly and SquareSpace integrate with Google Apps email to use your domain name with email as well.

You probably already thought about what domain name to choose when naming your business. And, hopefully you checked to see if it was available. If you didn't, do it now and cross your fingers! You can use the website building services above to check availability and register a domain or sites that focus on domains like Moniker (www.moniker.com).

If the domain you were hoping for is not available, taken by someone else, consider choosing a domain that includes a keyword phrase your business and products revolve around. For example, if your shop specializes in accessories made from real, natural sheep wool, but your shop name "Baa, Baa Black Sheep" is not available as a domain name (www.baabaablacksheep.com), then perhaps you can choose a domain that matches one of your products and helps people find you online, such as www.naturalwoolsweaters.com. Just because your shop name is not available as a dot com does not mean you have to come up with a new name, just get creative – you are great at that.

Search Engine Optimization

Key to being found online is appearing in search engine listings. This is likely the largest potential source of traffic. You want your website, blog or shop to rank as high as possible in search engine results so that you get more visitors to your website. To make your website rank higher, you need to choose the perfect keywords and phrases and use them to optimize your website. This process is called search engine optimization, abbreviated SEO. Finding the perfect keyword for your business takes time and a little know-how.

The first thing you will want to do is create a list of keywords and phrases that you think your customers will use to find your products. If you make wooden doll houses and furniture, one of your key phrases will be "wooden doll houses". Although, your potential customers may search many other keywords and phrases to find you – such as "dollhouses," "miniature doll houses," "miniature doll house furniture," "doll house furniture" and "wooden doll house miniatures". Think about all the different keywords and phrases that customers may use find your products. Put yourself in their shoes.

Next, head on over to Google's AdWords Keyword Analyzer Tool

JARGON ALERT

Have you seen those distorted letter and number combinations you have to enter and submit in order to log-in or post comments on many websites? That weird letter and number combination is known as a Captcha code. Websites use Captcha codes to ensure that a real human is logging into the website or posting the comment.

(adwords.google.com/select/keywordtoolexternal) and plug in your list of keywords and phrases that you wrote down before, enter the Captcha code and hit "Search". You will see a list of your keywords, along with their level of competition, and how often those keywords and phrases have been searched locally and globally in the last month. Brilliant!

If you scroll on down, you will notice an additional list of keyword ideas – suggested by Google – and their competition and monthly search numbers. Examine both lists and look for keywords with medium or low competition. Keywords with a lot of traffic but also a lot of competition are likely out of reach at this stage. Save focus on those for later on in your business growth once you are a bit more established. Be also cautious of phrases with low competition and low traffic. Even if you choose a low competition keyword and immediately raise your website to the number one result for that keyword, there may not be enough people searching for your keyword phrases to make a difference in sales.

Try to narrow in on one specific keyword or phrase to use as your main keyword. Use this as a guide when posting to your website, blog or store product descriptions. In simple terms, using this keyword phrase will help search engines find you and know what your site is about. And don't forget, as you scan your list of keywords and Google's suggested keywords for medium or low competition options, remember to check each keyword for correct spelling.

It is often helpful to include your main keyword in your website's tagline or in the first couple of sentences of your website, as those first few sentences show up with your url address in search engine results. At peaceloveglass, Laura Kelly's first line of text on her website is the tagline, "Stained glass art for your inner hippie". This is a great example of how Laura incorporated one of her keywords into the first line of text on her website.

Include the main keyword phrase and other keywords into the content on your website, from the home page, to the about page and even your contact page. However, it is incredibly important to not go overboard. There is no value in littering your text with repeated keywords or writing descriptions that make little sense only to scatter in a lot of prime keywords. In fact, search engines like Google can pick up on this and will likely de-value your site because of this practice. Instead, use your keyword phrases as guidance and direction when writing so you can keep in mind what your target audience is likely searching for, using keywords where they fit naturally.

Thanks to Google's early 2011 changes to their search engine algorithm, using your keywords organically in your text helps with search engine rankings and ensures that your copy is easy to read, entertaining and keeps your customers reading. If your copy is full of grammatical errors or is hard to read because you have stuffed too many keywords in – or reused one keyword too often – then your website rankings may be penalized, not to mention visitors may stumble over your content and decide to take their business elsewhere.

Blogging

Your blog is your business's soapbox. Step up and start talking about your creations and your business.

Blogging is a great way to connect with your target market and build a relationship with both new and existing customers. People are social creatures, so relationships and expressing your personality is incredibly important. Additionally, blogging helps improve your search engine rankings, particularly when you are updating often and including relevant keywords in your posts that will help your potential consumers find your blog – and through your blog find your shop and products.

Building a blog is not as complicated as you might think, so don't let this intimidate you. In fact, the website hosting service you use to create or host your business's standalone website may have a blogging feature built in. But, if not, you can create a free blog on WordPress (www.wordpress.com), Blogger (www.blogger.com) or Tumblr (www.tumblr.com) and link it to your website.

Then take time to learn about the blogging platform you are using. Watch tutorials on YouTube (www.youtube.com) and read online articles about your platform. Play around and familiarize yourself with the platform and learn how to write and publish blog posts.

At Originl, we hope to help you avoid the step of creating a standalone blog by allowing you to create and host your blog on our website, alongside your shop. This option takes the extra work out of promoting your blog, since our website already attracts traffic from consumers looking for creative articles, products and ideas.

There is no doubt in the business of being found online, content is king. Your blog posts should portray your voice and what you write about should be familiar and relevant to your target market. In the beginning, you'll have to generalize your target market, but as your business and blog grows – and you learn more about your target market – you can tailor your blog posts to meet your audience's tastes.

Gather ideas for what to include in your blog updates by researching other craft blogs that have a target market similar to yours. Pay attention to what sorts of posts they write and which of their posts generate the most comments and response from their readers. Take note of the voice they portray in their blog posts and what it tells you about their business; does it make their business appeal to you or does it fail to grab your attention? Remember to be true to your brand.

Write your blog posts to tell your consumers what projects you are working on, share free project instructions and share news about your business. This is a great way to break through the distance and let your fans get to know you and your personality as well as promote your products. Just avoid sounding too sales-y or too personal in your blog updates or you may lose your readers' interest. At the end of blog posts, invite your customers to participate in conversation about the topics in your posts via comments. This helps you build a relationship with your customers and readers and having a friendly relationship with others can encourage sales.

Blogging takes time, and it's probably not realistic for you to update your blog every day. This is perfectly ok. Blogging at lesser intervals can actually improve readership, making each post a bit more special. At least once per week or two is best. Avoid abandoning your blog for more than a month, especially if you have several followers. If you are not posting often enough or you tend to forget about your blog for months at a time, you will have trouble keeping your audience interested in what you have to say. To save time and avoid hassle, write several blog posts one slow afternoon and schedule them in advance for the next few weeks.

Google Analytics

Once you have your web presence and blog up and running, you will want to start tracking the results of your efforts and which keywords are generating the most traffic for your website. This will allow you to tweak your original keyword choices to fit the search habits of your target audience and boost your search engine rankings for those keywords that get the most traffic.

Start analyzing the traffic to your website and blog by signing up, for free, at Google Analytics (analytics.google.com). You will need to enter a unique code that Google generates for you into your webpages. This feature is often integrated in popular website building services. Within hours of setting it up, you will start to see data about your site and visitors and which keywords draw them to your page. The amount of information is amazing and critical to understanding the success of your SEO efforts. This will give you information about your visitors as well as help you focus on using those most successful keywords more often on your website and in blog posts.

14 PROMOTING YOUR BUSINESS ONLINE

With your website or blog in place to passively market your business and help your potential customers find you, it's time to start actively marketing your business and finding customers. There are so many avenues for promotion online it may at first seem like a daunting task. What should your first steps be when attempting to appeal to potential customers and draw them in to purchase your products?

This chapter outlines several different ways to actively promote your creative work in the online world. While there is no one right or wrong way, read through these techniques and pick a few to get started.

Guest Blogging

If you are just starting your own blog, it will take some time to build a strong readership. To shortcut this process and promote your business and products, you can guest blog on other craft blogs. Search and check out general craft sites and blogs in your specific craft medium. Look at how many readers the blog has – if that information is published – or visit the blog's social media profiles to see how many fans and followers exist. You can also gauge the blog's audience size based on how many comments the blog's posts get on average. When you find blogs related to your art or crafting niche with more than ten readers – but preferably over 50 or 100 readers – find their contact information and send them an email to ask if you could pitch a guest blog post. If those blogs ever do posts featuring different shops, ask if they would like to feature you and send over some samples of your work, along with a little bio about you and your products.

When you get an invitation to write a guest blog post, be cautious to not overly promote yourself. Write about how to create one of your crafts, or share your ideas on other crafts you make that you do not sell. The article should offer value to the readers as well as the owner of the blog. Avoid talking about your products much and never say, "you can buy my products here," and then link them to your shop or website. Instead, leave a link, short bio and a photo of one or two of your products at the end of the post or article. This prevents you from looking like a pushy advertiser. By posting information other crafters can use, you gain credibility and people who find your posts entertaining or educational will share them with their friends and often come visit your shops.

Listing in Online Directories

Help buyers find you by listing your business in key online business directories. Consider directories that are both global as well as local. Recent advancements in search engines as well as mobile devices make searching the web for local listings more relevant and useful. There are a number directory sites to choose from. Some of the most popularly used and those you will want to list your business on include the following.

- **Yahoo! Shopping** (shopping.yahoo.com)
- **Google Merchant Center** (www.google.com/merchants)
- **Google Places** (www.google.com/places)
- **Yahoo! Local Listings** (listings.local.yahoo.com)
- **CitySearch** (www.citysearch.com)
- **AOL's CityGuide** (www.aolmedianetworks.com)
- **MerchantCircle** (www.merchantcircle.com)
- **YellowPages** (www.yellowpages.com)

The process to get listed varies for each online directory. Some directories are free to list on, while others charge a fee. Many directories have the option to place a basic listing for free and offer options to upgrade to an advanced, paid listing, that allows you to list more about your business, including a collection of photos. Visit each online directory and browse around to see which directories are best for your business and fit your budget. Then list in as many directories as you can to reach a larger audience.

As you set up these accounts, fill out your profiles or listing completely (or fill out all that you can with a basic listing). If the directory allows you to write a bio about your business, write one and include the main keyword that consumers use to find your business. If the online directory services you choose provide the option, include a list of keywords that customers may enter into search engines to find you.

Actively promoting your creative business on other blog sites as well as online directories are great ways to build on your passive traffic generation from search engines. As you combine these and other techniques we will discuss next, you will begin to see increases in the visitor traffic to your website, blog and store. This blended approach adds layers of marketing channels rather than relying on just a single approach. As more and more people find you and learn who you are and what you do, the greater you will expand your brand's visibility.

Building both your brand as well as the number of people exposed to your products will ultimately increase your success in business.

15 NETWORKING AND SOCIAL MEDIA

Prepare to become a social butterfly.

One of the most recent and powerful ways to actively promote your business and brand online is to jump on your computer and start talking. Talk about your craft, talk about the inspiration behind your creations, talk about why you think your art will enlighten others – just start talking. And not just to your buyers, talk to other creatives (who are also consumers) – about your craft. Talk about news topics relevant to others in your space, talk about entrepreneurship, talk about marketing and taking the best product photos.

All this virtual talking and connecting with others is called social networking, and the more you do it, the more you will be "heard" and found online in conversation. This is another important technique to add to your blended approach to marketing.

Let's explore some of types of online venues you can use to join the discussion already in progress.

Community Sites

Community sites specifically focused in the art, craft and design space are great places to reach interested audiences. Craftser (www.craftster.com), Craft Juice (www.craftjuice.com), Get Crafty (www.getcrafty.com) and our own Originl (www.originl.com) offer communities for crafters to connect and talk about their trades. You can even join in conversation about business practices – ask advice and give advice on how to improve products, ways to market and every other thing you can think of that has to do with being a creative business owner.

When you are networking with other crafters, you build your credibility as a reliable source for creative business information and tips in your trade and you make friends who support what you do. And when people are interested in you and trust you as a source for information, they will check out your products. They may even become customers or share your products with their fans and followers.

Being found by only a few key people in your niche that are highly connected and highly vocal can be incredibly valuable for you and your business. If you can connect with a few of these unique individuals and begin to come up in their conversations as well as the conversations of their connections, the result is exponential. The resulting "viral" spread of a brand has resulted in more than a few businesses becoming overnight successes. These creative mavens are often found in online communities discussing what they are most passionate about.

Forums

Similar to community sites, forums offer a place to chat about topics relevant to you and your creative niche and do a bit of marketing for your business and products. Jump on your favorite search engine and start looking for forums. Look for forums in your craft industry, general craft forums, and forums for key members of your target market. For example, if your products are for babies or new and expectant mothers, look for parenting forums, forums about nursery decorating or pregnancy. Creative community sites like those we just covered also often include forums.

Create an account on the forum, typically free, and see what other members are talking about. Search for conversation topics where you have relevant knowledge or where you can market your business without looking like a spammer. For example, if there is a forum discussion about baby shower gift ideas, then jump in and mention your products and post a couple of pictures. Do not leave the same message and photos as a comment on every forum thread, only promote your products where relevant.

Join in conversation anywhere you have some relevant knowledge to offer. Remember that offering value in the content and discussions you post online is key to being read and appreciated. Always remember to include a short bio about what you do and links back to your website or shop at the end of your posts.

Associations and Societies

If any associations and societies exist in your crafting or art area of expertise, join them. Some will require paid subscriptions or memberships, while others offer free access. Connect with other members in groups or forums and enter your products into contests and showcases, when applicable. Associations also typically have regular meetings or local groups which are great ways to connect and network in person.

These societies are typically specific to a medium or geography, so I won't include an exhaustive list here. However, you can typically find those relevant to you with a quick web search. A few good lists to browse can also be found at artshow.com/orgs and sugarloafcrafts.com/guilds.html.

Social Media

Yes, this is the same social media where you connect with friends and friends of friends, watch your high school classmates' kids grow up, see what your co-workers did last night that made them late for work today and even tag photos of your family. They are also great ways to promote your creative products and raise awareness about your business.

Not only does engagement in social media help your business and products meet a larger audience of consumers, it also helps you build relationships with customers. Your social media profiles can even become a revenue stream, as new or existing customers contact you directly through your social media profiles to place orders for your products.

Be cautious that conducting business through your personal social media profile does not look professional. If you've got fans and followers on social networks that know you through your products, they don't want to wade through your personal pictures or read your personal status updates. They just want to see and read what is relevant to them as a potential buyer – photos and information about your products and your trade, or craft and business advice. So, take the time to create an account or page specific to your creative venture.

You will also want to allot time for updating and managing your social profiles. A page or profile with no relevant updates will not remain interesting to followers and not benefit your marketing efforts. The good news is, there are a number of ways you can integrate and automate your updates to manage multiple social media venues without a lot of additional effort. A service like HootSuite (www.hootsuite.com) is a very effective tool to automate posting to multiple social media platforms. With HootSuite, you can post to several accounts at once or even automate posting from an RSS feed or other source.

Now, there are many different social media outlets to choose from, but you will probably want to concentrate on the main two: Facebook and Twitter, in addition to any other social media outlets that are especially popular in the creative industry or among your friends and target market. Signing up is easy, but here are a few pointers and factors to keep mind to optimize your use of the two most popular social media outlets.

Facebook

Facebook (www.facebook.com) is the undeniable winner in the social network space. With such an incredibly large number of people already on Facebook, it should be part of your social marketing strategy.

To get started with Facebook, you will want to build a Facebook business or fan page for your business. Log onto your personal Facebook account and locate the option to "Create a Page". This option lets you access your page with the same log-in as your personal Facebook account. Facebook has a real name policy which prohibits you from creating a separate login under a fake name. Your fan page for your business will be separate from your personal profile and will not be publically linked unless you choose to. This also makes management of your business fan page or pages easy. If you do not yet have a Facebook account, simply fill out the few required fields on the Facebook home page and create your free account.

Next, choose a category and niche for your fan page based on Facebook's options and which option best describes your business and products. Fill out your fan page profile and title your page with your business name, product or combination thereof. Write a short bio about you, your business and your products, taking your time to carefully craft prose that makes you look professional and holds your reader's interest. Keep your defined target keyword phrases in mind while doing this. Include your email, business phone number and any other information you find relevant to share with your existing and potential customers.

Add photo albums to showcase your products and plan to add future pictures to show off new products or special, custom orders unlike other products in your shop. As you create new products, post them to your page along with descriptions, techniques or what makes them so unique. This is how you will interest potential fans and followers.

Once your business page is complete, be sure to make timely updates to your page so visitors will experience who you are as a designer. This is a great way to engage with existing and potential customers and get feedback to help hone your craft. Link to and from your page on your website, blog and shop to drive circular traffic among your different online promotional tools.

Steps to set up a Facebook page for your business:

1. Login to Facebook with your personal account. If you don't yet have one, create one by entering the basic required information at facebook.com.

2. Go to www.facebook.com/pages and click on the button to "Create Page".

3. Choose the type of page you wish to create and then select the category from the options provided.

4. Fill in the basic information requested through the setup wizard. A tutorial follows to introduce you to your new page.

5. Enter additional information about your business or brand by clicking on the "manage" button at any time.

6. Post photos, updates and links to your products. You can access your page in the future by finding it under the "Pages" section of your account or act as your business with the "Use facebook as" feature from your account dropdown menu.

7. Promote your new Facebook page with friends and customer and stay active with ongoing updates.

Twitter

Twitter (www.twitter.com) is another great promotional channel, albeit likely less understood by most. Twitter is a much more fluid communication tool that allows you to communicate openly with an incredibly large audience as well as customize what types of communications you receive, based on topic interests called "hash-tags" (#tag).

Create an account on Twitter and try to match your Twitter profile name (@name) with your business name. If you cannot get an exact match, keep searching for variations until you find the closest match available. Twitter names, much like domain names, are unique and available on a first come first served basis. Consider adding the suffix "tweet" to a shortened version of your business name as an option such as @originltweet. Or, consider using a tagline or company slogan as your account name to further build your brand.

Set up your business's Twitter account using any email address – your personal email, the email address hooked to your website or a generic email you set up through Yahoo, Gmail or another email provider for your business. Fill out your profile information and upload a picture such as your logo or a photo of your most popular product, so that you look like a real business.

Then, use Twitter's search bar to start searching for other crafters to connect with. You can search with free text or for specific topics using hash-tags. Find other creatives you find interesting and "follow" them. This will include their posts into your Twitter account feed, so you will see their communications (tweets). People you follow will be notified which may typically lead to them following you back or checking out your website and engage in conversation with you.

As you follow more people and get more comfortable with Twitter, you can re-tweet interesting posts by others. This pushes out their communications into your feed and thus seen by your followers. Your followers can in turn re-tweet your tweets thereby pushing out your message to a larger audience. Twitter is also often integrated into blogs and other websites and display tweets specific to the topic of the site. As you can quickly see, this is a very powerful medium.

Generate even more Twitter followers by using hash-tags. Start by searching that list of keywords you made in the Be Found Online chapter on Twitter's search feature. Add a hash tag or pound symbol (#) at the beginning of each of your keywords - #oilpainting, #customnurseryart, #holidaycrafts etc. – and look to see how much those keywords have been talked about recently on Twitter. Follow others talking about those keywords if you think that person is a potential customer or a fellow creative that you can network with. If any of your keywords are getting a lot of talk, take note so you can be sure to include those specific hash-tags into your future tweets. Any Twitter users that are interested in, "following," those specific hash-tag topics will then see your communications, even if they are not following you.

You should also check out the trending topics and hash-tags displayed on the right-hand side of your Twitter home page. If you can fit any of those popular phrases and hash-tags into your next Tweet, do it – this helps your Tweets reach a larger audience so that people can follow you without you making the first move to find them. But, always remember to keep your tweets high quality and relevant.

Social Bookmarking

As the name implies, social bookmarking is an online technique for organizing and sharing websites that you enjoy or want to reference later. Two of the more popular social bookmarking services, StumbleUpon (www.stumbleupon) and Pinterest (www.pinterest.com), offer a downloadable toolbar for your web browser. From the browser, as you are visiting websites, you can give the website a thumbs up or down rating or "pin" it to your pin boards. Thumb down ratings help StumbleUpon know not to show you similar pages in the future. However, thumbs up rankings and pins are what are relevant to your business's use of these sites. Give your website, shop, blog and each new blog post a thumbs up or pin to help in promotion.

If you have friends using StumbleUpon or Pinterest, the sites you like will be shared amongst your friends. Even if you do not have friends using these sites, giving your own site a mention will help you build back links and achieve higher engine rankings. Be sure to thumbs up and pin other shops, craft blog posts and products to help build your credibility.

StumbleUpon and Pinterest are not your only options; there are many social bookmarking sites to choose from. Search for any that may be more relevant to your craft field and experiences, or focus on the more popular bookmarking sites like Digg (www.digg.com), Reddit (www.reddit.com) and Delicious (www.delicious.com).

Social media is not just for friends anymore. These sites offer very powerful channels to reach incredibly large populations that can become important contacts in your business, cross-promoters and customers. Consider your social media strategy seriously as effective use of these tools can dramatically increase your marketing success.

Take Action!

☑ **Create a Facebook page for your brand.**

Create a business page on Facebook for your creative business. Upload product photos and descriptions and be sure to link back to your online store.

☑ **Start tweeting.**

Create an account on Twitter named after your company or product name. Start tweeting to give relevant updates or join related conversations.

16 PROMOTING YOUR BUSINESS OFFLINE

Maybe it sounds old fashioned, but just because your business is online, doesn't mean you have to reserve all your marketing measures for cyberspace. There are hundreds of promotional opportunities waiting for you every time you walk out your front door.

Some methods of offline promotion will put you in direct contact with potential customers so you can show off your personality, build relationships with potential and existing customers and make sure your shoppers remember you and your products. Other offline promotion methods may not put you in direct contact with buyers, but will help you market your products to a large audience. And some offline promotions will do both – putting you in direct contact with a large audience of new potential customers.

Here are some key ways to start promoting your business and products through offline venues.

Art & Craft Shows

This should be an obvious way to promote your products offline and engage in direct contact with buyers. In fact, many artists and crafters start attending craft fairs long before they start selling their products online. That doesn't mean you have to start this way, or that you even have to fit an art or craft show into your busy schedule, but it is definitely a great way to display your products to an interested audience.

You may have to pay a booth fee to set up at an arts and craft show, but you will be able to sell your products at these shows and even meet other creative business owners and hobbyists to network with. Plus, you get a chance to talk directly to potential buyers and, if you listen to what your customers say about your products, you may even get ideas for future products. When attending their local craft fair, Jessica and Susan Partain of Inedible Jewelry like to question their younger buyers for ideas on new foods they could use as models for future charms.

If there's not an organized fair in your local town, look for one at a nearby tourist location. This way you will not only get attention to your shop from area locals, but also from out-of-towners from around the globe. You may also look for local clubs related to your specific craft. These will likely be aware of nearby shows or may host events themselves which you may not yet have identified.

Guest Books

Make the most of your time spent at fairs or shows by getting buyers, and even those shoppers that don't buy, to sign a guest book. A guest book is simply a sheet of paper or journal with their names, email addresses and other contact information. You can use this list later to send out occasional newsletters for your business. This is a great way to stay connected with potential buyers that did not convert during the limited time of the show. Just be sure you offer a way for individuals to unsubscribe to your mailings if they decide not to receive them and do not email too often. Once or twice a monthly is plenty.

Encourage more people to sign up on your guest list and give their email addresses to you by giving away one of your products or a gift certificate code to use in your online shop. Then, generate more followers on your social media profiles by inviting everyone

SNEAK PEEK

We will talk more about email etiquette in the following chapter, Building Relationships with Buyers.

who signs up to follow you on Twitter or fan you on Facebook where you will reveal the giveaway winner.

Business Cards or Art Cards

Never leave home without a few business cards. And if you are headed to an art and craft show, bring along a whole stack, and pass them out to everyone. If you do not yet have business cards, this should be a top priority.

You can design and order business cards at Vistaprint (www.vistaprint.com), Moo (www.moo.com) or make them yourself using a business card template on your word processing program and card stock paper or specialty business card printer paper. As you design your card, remember to make it match your brand and personality. You do not need to list all your contact information nor do

TIP

Use the same product photo that is on your business card as your profile pictures on Twitter and Facebook so there is no way your customers can confuse you with other fan pages and profiles with names similar to yours.

127

you want dull cards that fail to make an impact on recipients. Design your cards to include only basic information others need to find your online shops and website, such as your website address and how to find you on Twitter or Facebook. And if you can, include your logo or place a photo of one of your products on your business cards so that every time someone looks at your cards they will be reminded or your beautiful, creative pieces.

Cards are also great to include with products you sell. When your customers or their friends are in the market for something new, your card will be there to remind them where to find you.

Take Your Products Everywhere You Go

While not the best option for furniture or large items, if your creative products are wearable or functional, take them with you everywhere you go. From running personal errands at the bank to picking up recipe ingredients at the grocery store, simply wearing your products or having an example with you can be an effective tool. When someone compliments one of your wearable products, smile, thank them politely while handing them one of your business cards. "I made it myself. I'm a professional artisan, and you can visit my website if you want to see more of my creations." If they liked your product enough to compliment a complete stranger, then chances are high they will check out your site and shop.

Magazines & Newspapers

Get your products featured in both online and print magazines and local newspapers by sending an email or post mail letter to the newspaper's editor, or the department of the magazine where your creative product will fit in. Submit high-resolution photos and written descriptions of your products and ask if the publication would be interested in doing an article about you (newspapers) or including your products in "top ten" lists or recommended product spreads (magazines). Offer to send a free piece if they want to stage photos for their publications.

Submit your pitches to magazines several months ahead of season. Many major publications work on strict timelines on issues and you may need to submit seasonal items, like Christmas ornaments, 6 months before the magazine's winter or December issue is meant to hit the shelves.

> ## JARGON ALERT
>
> Submitting product updates and information about your business to newspapers in order to generate some free publicity is called submitting a **press release**.

You're not limited to submitting your products to crafts, fashion or home-decorating magazines. Think about the designs on your products, what your product is used for. If your products are for babies, submit photos to parenting magazines. If you have crafty products for pets, submit to pet magazines. If you make wedding fashions and accessories, submit to wedding magazines. Yoga themed jewelry? Share them with yoga magazines. And if you're up for selling and shipping internationally, try submitting to magazines in other countries; just try to stick to countries with languages you are familiar with, unless you know a good translator.

You might not end up with your products featured in the print-versions of these publications, but mention in an online article on their site is just as noteworthy and helps generate shop traffic.

If you never hear back from the publication, maybe your products were not a great fit at the time, but that doesn't mean the editor won't remember your products and decide to use your photos later. Plus, you can always pitch again at a later date.

Make Donations

Know of a local charity that is hosting an auction or raffle to raise money? Give them one of your products and call it a business expense. Similarly, donate your pieces to local businesses that don't mind displaying your products and see if you can include a small sign or business card display for people to take and look you up online later. Do not donate to retail shops and consignment stores, instead think of different businesses. Restaurants, coffee shops, business lobbies and other locations may be great places to showcase your artwork and generate free publicity.

Give one of your creations to your favorite bank teller and ask her to display it on her desk and notify you when your display runs out of business cards. See if your doctor's office would be willing to place one of your appropriate decorative items on their reception desk. The possibilities of places to donate and get free advertising for your products are only as limited as your supply of pieces you are willing to give away. Just pick the places that make the most sense to you, your target consumers and your product.

Shops & Consignment

Another great way to promote your products offline and even create another revenue stream is to sell your product to and at local craft and gift shops and galleries. You can even sell to out-of-town or out-of-state shops if you are willing to travel to sell your products in-store. However, for this marketing measure, you may have to raise your regular prices to ensure both you and the businesses selling your products make a profit.

> **JARGON ALERT**
>
> Selling your arts and crafts on **consignment** means you give them to shops at no cost and get paid when your products sell.

Also, different shops have different guidelines for selling your products. While some may be willing to buy your products and require a reimbursement for items that do not sell, other shops may require that you consign your products. This means they only pay you when your items sell.

Take Action!

☑ **List offline promotion sources.**

Create a list of regional or national art and craft fairs, consignment shops or retail establishments where you can display or sell your creations. Be sure to include contact details and any notes on fees or special requirements.

☑ **Get business cards.**

Have some simple but nice looking business cards printed and use them in your offline networking. Include them with products you sell or display locally.

17 BUILDING RELATIONSHIPS WITH BUYERS

How did you get your most recent job? How did you meet your significant other? From where did you learn about the car you drive or the recipe you made for dinner last?

Relationships are paramount. They are the foundation of any successful venture. We discussed previously the importance of networking and marketing communications as a part of promoting your brand. As these efforts start to translate into more traffic, you are presented with an opportunity and challenge to engage with visitors. Connecting with and building strong relationships with your buying community will become key to increasing sales and developing repeat customers.

Building relationships with your buyers helps them feel a connection with you. Shoppers looking for unique hand crafted items are often looking for this type of connection with the artisan. While you will likely not become fast friends, buyers who feel they really know who you are and what you stand for are more likely to share you with their own friends on social networks. It is much more frequent they will give the back story on your hand crafted item when admired by their family and friends. When this happens, you can rely less heavily on your active marketing efforts and watch your bottom line continue to rise.

The benefits of taking time to build a relationship with your buyers do not stop there. By engaging with your potential customers and existing buyers – on social media, in the comments on your blog, via email and any other way you connect to consumers – you can learn about your target market and narrow your business's focus to fit your customers.

Communicating with your buyers helps you see what motivates them to buy your products, gives you ideas for new products and provides you with feedback you can use to improve your existing products. This is incredibly important to not overlook. The good news is, there are many tools and outlets to assist you.

Engage Fans and Followers

Indulge your inner rock star and use social platforms to build a loyal fan base. But focus less on how many fans and followers you have on your social media profiles or blog. If you are not engaging with those people, you will not see the value they can provide. The more followers you have the broader your marketing reach, but it is engaging with them that results in the most impactful results.

Let them in to what's going on in your world. Tell them what you are working on and what is currently inspiring you. If you experienced a great show or tried out a new technique, communicate this through your various channels. These fairly simple communications will be interesting to your followers and will help them get a better sense of your personality and style.

If you are only using your communications channels to

> **TIP**
>
> Become a fan or follower of other artists and crafters and examine their social media profiles to see how they are communicating and engaging with others. You might meet some great people too!

post updates about your business and what you are selling, you may come across as too sales-y and turn people away. Instead, talk about the history behind your creations and let people know through how you word your status updates and photo descriptions, just how passionate you are about what you do. Let your fans and followers in on what projects you are working on and ask them to give you feedback on new product ideas. This engagement makes them feel like they are part of something and that will keep them interested in your work.

Keep your audience in mind as you craft status updates and upload pictures of your creations. Think about how you can engage them in conversation with what you post. And when you get new fans and followers, take the time to scope out their profiles and see what they are into, then connect with them in a conversation about something – even if it's not about crafts or your products. If you like the same college basketball team, talk about that. There is no limit to what you can talk to them about, but avoid getting too personal. Try thanking them for becoming a fan and strike up a relevant conversation to let them know that your customers are of upmost importance to you. Remember that building relationships is not always about a single specific outcome in mind.

Email newsletters are another great way to communicate with and engage the buying community. Many website services include newsletter features which allow you to include a sign-up form on your website to

> ## QUOTE
>
> "I read somewhere – as I was teaching myself what I needed to know about starting my online stained glass art business – that if you want to get someone to subscribe to your newsletter, don't call it a newsletter. That's why I invite my customers to sign up for the 'Love List'."
>
> – Laura Kelly of peaceloveglass

collect additional email addresses of visitors. You can also use services like Constant Contact (www.constantcontact.com) to build a list and send out email newsletters or special communications.

Since signing up for your email newsletter is more of an active step for visitors over simply following your social profile or blog, it is a great sign they are very interested in what you do. Consider crafting your communications to this group a bit differently than your more public channels. Email communications to this list to update them on what you are creating and any other relevant information is an effective way to reach out to individuals that are not avid blog readers.

Finally, consider mentioning other crafters in your posts and communications as you find other creative people and products that inspire you. Tag them in your posts, so they get a little free publicity and maybe a few more fans. This helps you build a community. This collaborative interaction with other creatives will pay off as they will return the favor and share you amongst their connections.

Communicate Often, But Not Too Often
A Note on Can-Spam Compliance

Just because they sign up as fans and followers, subscribe to your blog posts, or sign up to your mailing list, does not mean that your buyers are giving you permission to spam their email inboxes or Facebook and Twitter feeds with updates. Limit yourself to two or three status updates per day maximum and spread them out throughout the day to catch them when they are getting their social media fix. Also try to avoid posting the same update multiple times.

The same goes for blog updates and email newsletters. Obviously, you will not be sending those out multiple times per day, but you probably should not even send them out multiple times per week. If you blog numerous times per week, consider setting up an option allowing readers to choose between notifications for every post or just weekly digest updates.

And unless there is a gift-giving occasion or you create a new product every week, there is simply no reason to be sending out email communications more than a few times per month. Once you start sending out numerous email newsletters with the same or similar content, your subscribers will quickly feel overwhelmed and unsubscribe from your list. Send out more lengthy email newsletters once a month or only once a quarter so you're not filling up your subscribing buyers inboxes.

Be careful not to craft your emails to sound like an advertisement. Instead, if you have products that would make great mother's day presents, then send out more targeted emails to your list and let them know if they are searching for a gift for their mothers you've got what they need. This slight difference turns an email from an advertisement into something of potential value to the recipient.

The concept of offering value is a key one to remember. Think about it each time you post an update or send a communication. Am I offering information of value to my list? If not, consider modifying. This will go a long way toward developing a devoted base.

Remember as well that all email lists must include an option to unsubscribe. The Can-Spam Act of 2003 includes a number of criteria that must be met for compliance. This includes the ability to unsubscribe from any opt-in email list such as your newsletter. It also includes requirements preventing false or misleading information in your subject line or from name and address. The bottom line is, be good to your email subscribers and you will both be respected and be obeying the law.

18 ADVERTISING AND AFFILIATES

By now you have a lot of great marketing tools in your creative toolbox. Once you have these low or no cost strategies in place, then it may be time to start an advertising campaign for your creative business. Advertising can help you reach a larger audience, across the nation or across the globe. As with the many marketing activities we have discussed, advertising can be an effective technique to add to your blended approach to promotion.

When you're first starting your creative business, you may be concerned that effective advertising is not within your budget. Don't be intimidated by the cost; you can find an advertising method that fits most any budget. This is especially true of online advertising. There are two main types of online advertising to choose from, and you can specify your budget on each when starting the campaigns.

With PPC (pay-per-click) advertising, you'll pay a specified dollar and cent amount for each click your ads receive. These clicks will lead customers to your website or shop and, with luck, will result in sales of your products. The amount you have to pay for each click depends upon the parameters you set while creating your advertising campaign. These parameters may include specifying the region, gender and ages of your target market. Additionally, you'll specify a list of keywords about your products and advertisement, so that your ad appears in search engines or on websites that include those same keywords.

The exact amount you'll pay for each click varies depending on these parameters and is often based on a bidding system. Most advertising programs allow you to set a range or limit on how much you are willing to pay for the entire campaign or for each click.

Placement in search engine results ads, for example, will give preference to advertisers that are willing to pay a higher amount per click for a specific keyword. Dropping the amount you are willing to pay for each click will reduce the amount of times your advertisements appear or lower your placement in the list; you get what you pay for. The good news is, you don't necessarily need to be number one on the list. Consider looking at the estimated placement of your ad when building your campaign and determine the best bid price that gets you near the top while not breaking your budget or over-paying for a slightly better placement.

Your second option, CPM advertising – which stands for cost-per-mille – requires that you pay a fee for every 1,000 impressions your ads generate. (Mille is Latin for 1,000). Impressions are each time your advertisement is viewed, not necessarily clicked. With this online advertising method, you can choose the websites on which your ads will be listed and what you will pay for every 1,000 times your advertisement is loaded on those websites. Know that these systems are quite smart and do not over-charge you for duplicate impressions, so don't worry about page reloads or internal user action of website owners trying to run up your impression count to make more money off hosting your advertisements.

The CPM option is a good way to get more broad exposure to larger numbers of people than just those that actively click on links in your ads. Both banner and text advertisements are available under this model and are comparable to billboards. Even if a viewer does not actually click on your ad, you may get some residual branding benefit.

Google AdWords

Popular search engine and Internet giant, Google, offers its own online advertising network so you can start advertising online in minutes – or at least in a few hours. Many different businesses use Google AdWords (adwords.google.com) as a key part of their advertising strategy. You will want to do a little research and get really specific with your advertising to get the highest return on advertising investment. But if you are willing to do the leg work, Google provides you with text, display, online video and even TV ad campaigns you may display in search engines, on websites and in on-air television.

With both PPC and CPM advertising models available through Google, and given that the Google search engine is the undeniable leader in this space, this is definitely a good place to start advertising. Google also typically offers first time coupons for $50 or $100 in advertising budget to get started, so look for those offers. AdWords also integrates with Google Analytics for a complete view of how your advertising campaigns result in traffic and ultimately sales. As you try out a few different types of ad campaigns, monitor the results in the reporting tool available through Google and adjust as needed.

> **JARGON ALERT**
>
> **ROI** is an acronym for return-on-investment. Having a high return on investment means you are making the most of the time and money you are spending.

Microsoft adCenter

Advertise on Yahoo! Search (www.yahoo.com) and Bing (www.bing.com) using the centralized Microsoft adCenter platform (advertising.microsoft.com/small-business). Ad campaigns are easy to set up at Microsoft adCenter, and their service even crawls your website to suggests which keywords to use to maximize your advertising ROI.

You will be able to set bids on the dollar and cent amounts you are willing to pay for each click your ads receive. You may bid as low as 5 cents, though Microsoft adCenter recommends you bid at least 30 cents per click to ensure your ads get visibility. They suggest that bidding higher gives you a competitive advantage over other advertisers using your keywords. Although Microsoft adCenter has a slightly more simple ad creation process than Google, they do not offer display banner ads, so you have to create ad copy that invites consumers to visit your website to see your products.

Facebook Ads

With everyone – including your mother – on Facebook (www.facebook.com) these days, you would be amiss not to at least give Facebook advertising a try. Your ads appear on the right-hand side of a user's screen when they are using any of Facebook's pages and are fully customizable to fit your target market and your budget. You can even choose between linking your advertising to your Facebook fan page or to your website address. Additionally, you can include photos in your ad at no extra cost and specify that ads only appear to consumers that are not already fans of your business's Facebook page.

Affiliate Programs

You can even choose to pay other people to promote your business on their own websites and through their social media profiles using affiliate programs. These programs can sometimes be seen at the center of less scrupulous Internet product marketing, but they are a powerful way of multiplying your sales force. So, consider giving these a try as you expand your business sales channels.

Popular services that coordinate affiliate networks include those offered by ClickBank (www.clickbank.com) and Commission Junction (www.cj.com). You can also set up an affiliate program through other niche sites. At the core of an affiliate program is an agreement to pay your affiliate a fee or percentage of sales they refer to your store. While most services allow your affiliate advertisers to take a commission percentage for all sales that result from their efforts, others require that you pay either for clicks or impressions – PPC and CPM.

Advertising in the Real World

While online advertising is typically the most cost effective way of driving traffic to your online store, you are not limited to advertising only online. If your creative products will appeal to local consumers, you may also try advertising in local print publications, such as your local newspaper or magazines specific to your state or town – or even magazines in your specific craft industry or a general crafting magazine. If your budget allows, and you can advertise effectively in these markets, you may also try radio and television advertising for your creative products. However, I suggest these options only for special events or as your business grows substantially.

19 PAYMENT AND SHIPPING

Once your shop is up and running and your marketing efforts are driving shoppers to you, you'll need to know how to navigate the payment and shipping process of closing sales. While a necessary logistical step, there are also important opportunities to build your service and brand.

Accepting Payment

Most online shops, from Etsy to Shopify – and even our own Originl – process credit and debit card payments for you. This typically means there's no need to establish a merchant account or separate payment processing service as you would with a brick and mortar store.

Payment processing almost always includes using the globe's most popular money transfer service, PayPal (www.paypal.com). Since so many different sites process order payments with this service, PayPal is likely the best option to use to manage all your online revenue streams in one place. It's free and easy to sign up for PayPal, and you can even accept credit cards directly if your customers are not already PayPal members. You will, however, have to pay PayPal processing fees on transactions, but these are typically only slightly higher than standard credit card processing fees.

PayPal also offers additional merchant services that allow you to manage other aspects of your business. Using Paypal's Merchant Services, you can export your sales and payment information, pay for and print shipping labels and even add "Buy Now" buttons to your website if not using a selling platform.

But what if you're selling on location at an art or crafts fair? You don't want to be limited to just accepting cash and you may be weary of accepting checks. To accept credit cards on location, you can use the Square app (www.square.com) and card-reader attachment that plugs into the headphone jack of your iPad, iPhone or Android. You can download the Square app for free and when you sign up, Square will ship you their card reader attachment at no-cost. When you are ready to accept a payment, simply enter the purchase price and swipe your customer's card. You will be charged a processing fee of 2.75% for each sale and funds will automatically transfer to your bank account the next day. Note that if you have to enter credit card numbers manually, Square will charge a larger rate of 3.5% of the transaction, plus 15 cents.

If you are selling on location, you will also want to remember to charge state sales taxes on your purchases or prepare to deduct that amount from your profit to pay your business's sales taxes. And of course, keep good records.

Shipping

Shipping your purchased creations to their new home is typically the last step in the sales process and your last chance to make an impression on your customer. Pay attention to quality in this step just as you do in creating your products.

First, be sure to choose the correct shipping method and price it correctly. Even if your buyers do not pay you through PayPal, you can still use your Paypal Merchant Services tools to purchase and print shipping labels, which helps you avoid those long, time consuming lines at the local post office. If you are shipping items of various weights, you may find it also useful to invest in a digital postal shipping scale that prints exact priced labels for your packages.

When it comes to shipping and handling charges, be realistic. Don't sell your products for $5 and charge $20 in shipping and handling fees or charge outrageous shipping fees for tiny, light-weight items as a way of boosting your overall profit. Your customers can do the math, and this kind of pricing strategy can make them second-guess buying from you. However, if your products are fragile or expensive, you may need to charge higher shipping prices to purchase shipping insurance or ship first class to protect your products and ensure they reach their destination unharmed.

Finally, consider unique wrapping or packaging when shipping products. Who doesn't get excited when they see a blue box from Tiffany's! This is another opportunity to reinforce your brand with your packaging choices. For example, if you focus on eco-friendly creations, consider recycled packaging. If you sew or knit your products, consider tying up the wrapped product with a scrap of fabric or yarn.

Take Action!

☑   **Set up a PayPal account.**

If you don't already have a PayPal account for your business, create one and link it to your credit card or business checking account to begin accepting payments.

20 CUSTOMER SERVICE

As a small business owner, your customers are your biggest asset. Once you get them, you'll want to keep them. And you do this by not only building relationships with them and sharing information but also by providing outstanding customer service.

In fact, think of customer service as an extension of your brand. If your customers have questions – or engage with you in email, on the phone or on your social media profiles – take the time to listen to their needs and then respond promptly to let them know that you care about their inquiries. If a customer is unsatisfied with your product, or there is a problem with shipping, do what you can to make them happy. This is an incredibly important point I have learned in business and shouldn't be overlooked.

Very happy customers, just like very unhappy ones, will be vocal. They can just as easily tell their friends to avoid you or talk about how amazing your customer service is. Happy customers will recommend you every chance they get and act as brand ambassadors for your creative business. When you are devoted to customer service, you make your customers feel important and treasured. Knowing they are more to you than a dollar sign will result in repeat customers and a strong community that supports what you do.

If one of your customers calls you up out of the blue to complain that your product has broken due to a design flaw, ask them to send back the broken item, absorb the return-shipping costs and ideally send them a new, replacement piece for free. Then, examine the returned broken item to see how you can prevent the same problem from happening to future products and customers. Similarly, if there is an issue in which an item is lost in the mail, send out a new product even if it means you have lost money on one item. And always invest in shipping insurance when shipping overseas or shipping super expensive or fragile items that you cannot afford to replace if they are lost in shipping.

While you may lose a little profit on a few items or with a few customers, this approach will benefit you in the end as you build a solid reputation and devoted fans. After all, this is your dream career we're talking about. Let's build it with the respect and dedication it deserves.

Take Action!

☑ **Create customer service templates.**

To reduce the time burden of good customer service, create template responses to common requests. This can be as simple as a document stored on computer with examples you can copy and paste into email responses. Consider building a frequently asked questions (FAQ) page of your website or store to give answers to common questions.

21 TAKING THE NEXT STEP

Your creative business will most likely start out small and simple. If you follow the techniques in this book and devote yourself to hard-work and the occasional long work-day, it won't take you long to turn your business into a success. In fact, you may end up with more work than you can manage on your own. With luck, you'll be ready to move on to the next step and grow your business.

As you do this, first consider *if* you want to grow your business larger. For most entrepreneurs, the obvious answer is yes. But, as you grow, consider just how large you are interested in taking your business. Build this into your evolving business plan and know that there is no shame in deciding to stay small. This is a perfectly fine decision and by no account means that you are not successful. It was likely the characteristics of a small business that attracted you to this path in the first place.

Health Insurance

If you don't have a spouse with a corporate job to rely on for health insurance, then you are likely beginning to miss that benefits package you had at your last job. And like most, you could be terrified of what independent health insurance will cost you. You may have to scrape by for a few months without health insurance, which is certainly not ideal. Once you can build it into your business finances, consider adding health insurance for you and any other employees in your company.

One great option is to get your health insurance and other benefits through Freelancer's Union (www.freelancersunion.org). Freelancer's Union was created to help independent workers receive the same healthcare and additional benefits available to traditional employees at affordable prices. With membership in the Freelancer's Union, you can get health, dental, life and disability insurance, and even start a retirement plan. But also consider doing additional research and comparisons to find the best health insurance plan for your needs and budget.

Hiring Employees

When the day arrives that you are constantly busy filling orders and staying engaged with your customers, then it may be time to consider hiring a few employees. If you don't want to deal with the paperwork and hassle behind hiring a full- or part-time staff member, try outsourcing some of your tasks to freelancers or other small businesses. Hire an accountant to take care of your paperwork or pay your mother or your neighbor to help you package and ship products during your busy seasons. Craigslist (www.craigslist.com) is another great source for local hires and offers job postings for very low fees.

If you cannot find someone local to help you with book-keeping, marketing or another task that can be done remotely, then outsourcing virtually might be an option. Try posting a job advertisement on trusted freelancing sites like oDesk (www.odesk.com), Elance (www.elance.com) or Freelancer (www.freelancer.com).

You can even try out newer group based services called crowd sourcing. These sites allow you to post a project job such as creation of a marketing message or logo and have hundreds of people post potential options for you to consider before choosing one and paying the winner the agreed upon fee. Examples of these sites include Crowd Spring (www.crowdspring.com) and Squad Help (www.squadhelp.com). You may be surprised at how fast and inexpensive it is to access a wealth of talent.

Re-Stating Goals and Updating Your Business Plan

As your business grows, remember to take out your business plan and re-state your goals to fit your changing business. Typically once a year is a good interval to review your plan and update as necessary. It is an important step in keeping your business on track and monitoring your business's growth.

Whatever you do, stay focused on your company's vision and mission and your own values. It's easy to get bogged down in the day to day routine, but it's your initial business concept and creative passion that drew you to take this step. Keep your focus there.

22 CONCLUSION

I hope your creative business venture is now beginning to feel real. There's a lot of hard work required to turn your creative passions into a successful business and a strong brand. But, getting to do what you love is all the motivation you need.

There will be ups and downs as you get your business started, but hang in there – know you can do it.

With the experience to know what tools and ingredients are most effective in your journey, we designed our Originl creative network with you in mind. I invite you to join us at Originl.com where you can not only sell your products but also connect and build relationships with other crafters and potential customers. At Originl, you will be able to create online inspiration albums, publish updates and organize a portfolio of your work that other crafters and buyers can browse and comment on. And since Originl is purpose built for artists, crafters, designers and other creative folk, your Originl shop will enjoy traffic from shoppers looking specifically for handmade creations.

So, whether you are ready to begin selling or are just starting the process of defining your craft, I am confident you will love Originl.

Let us help you get started by opening your free account on Originl.com.

Now it's time to take action. I suggest referring back to the first few chapters in this book as your very next action step. Refresh on the importance of defining who you want to be as a creative business, your mission, what your core products are, your target audience and your brand.

There are so many options and you'll have so many ideas during this journey. Remember to stay focused and understand how your creative mind works. There are also so many avenues to market and sell your amazing creations. Start small and build with a blended approach. As you have successes, celebrate them. As you experience setbacks, do not be discouraged. Hard work and thoughtful persistence will be your key to success. You are a crafty entrepreneur.

CONTRIBUTER BIOGRAPHIES

Here at Originl, we would like to extend a special thank you to the artists and crafters who shared their experiences and hard-earned knowledge about running an online arts and crafts business successfully.

Heidi Ferguson, Honeybear Lane

www.honeybearlane.com

Craft enthusiast and owner of Honeybear Lane, Heidi Ferguson started her craft business on a whim; she simply wanted to see if she could make a little extra money selling her creations. She started out making flower clips, baby clothing, skirts and baby bedding. Today, she primarily sells patterns and kits for her unique, snuggly Puff Quilts. Heidi is also a devoted blogger, using her business blog to inspire others to harness their creativity, gain crafting confidence and learn about the handmade business.

Stacey Gordon, Puppet Pie

www.etsy.com/shop/staceyrebecca

Storyteller and puppet master Stacey Rebecca Gordon has been designing puppets and practicing the imaginative art of puppetry since April 2002. She continues to perform with and make hand puppets, rod puppets and finger puppets that include animals, insects, flowers and foods for folks of all ages to enjoy.

Kevin and Shawn Hull, Hull's Happiest Days Designs

www.happiestdaysdesigns.com

From their farmhouse studio in the Pennsylvania countryside, husband and wife, Kevin and Shawn Hull create functional and artistic dessert ware that pays tribute to the happiest moments in their customer's lives. Each of their designs is hand-drawn and then carefully transferred and hand-applied to dessert ware pieces and may commemorate special days and moments such as buying a new home, weddings, anniversaries, holidays and birthdays.

Jenny Jafek-Jones, The Crimson Poppy

www.thecrimsonpoppy.com

Jenny Jafek-Jones's craft business was born when she was scouring the Internet looking for paper flower tutorials to make a floral arrangement for her wedding. She discovered the fascinating art of kusudama origami, and quickly set to work deconstructing real flowers to learn all she could about making beautiful and realistic flowers from paper. Her long-lasting floral arrangements are perfect for any occasion and recommended for other out there, who - like Jenny - harbor "black thumbs".

Jackie Kaufman, Rock My World
www.etsy.com/shop/rockmyworldinc

Jewelry designer and silver-caster, Jackie Kaufman, of Rock My World uses the lost art of wax casting to carve intricate molds for her one-of-a-kind sterling silver jewelry. In addition to creating detailed wax molds of Buddha and tiny owls, Jackie also produces cast necklaces using molds of fingerprints, thumbprints, paw prints and pet noses that serve as both keepsakes and beautiful wardrobe accessories.

Laura Kelly, peaceloveglass
www.peaceloveglass.com

Stained glass artist, Laura Kelly, owner of peaceloveglass spent 15 years working in the corporate world before taking a stained glass class that changed her life. She started out as a hobbyist making pieces to gift to friends but she now spends her days creating and selling beautiful stained glass art that is calming, inspirational and just makes people feel good.

Lauren Kilbourne, The Littlest Feather
www.etsy.com/shop/thelittlestfeather

Full-time student and part-time nanny, Lauren Kilbourne, owner of The Littlest Feather made her first set of whimsical, feather earrings for her sister as a birthday present. With encouragement from her friends, Lauren began selling her creations online shortly after. Although she's still in school, she continues to make her feathered jewelry, and she loves it so much she's considering changing her major and turning her jewelry-making venture into a full-time career.

Alexandra Koiv, Alex in Welderland's Custom Pet Urns

www.custompeturns.com

Alexandra Koiv has always been a metal sculpture artist, but her creative business, Alex in Welderland's Custom Pet Urns was not born until a friend asked her to create a pet urn for his beloved, recently passed cat. That's when the light-bulb above her head lit up and she decided to combine her love of pets and desire to help people with her creative talents to create her pet urn business.

Nikki McGonigal, Nikki, In Stitches

www.nikkiinstitches.com

Nikki McGonigal – owner of Nikki, In Stitches – started her crafting career as a blogger, encouraging and empowering others to experiment with their creativity. After a year and a half of blogging, she decided it was time to turn her blog into a business and started selling craft books, kits, patterns and a few finished creative products. She continues to add new inventory to her online shops and has a dream of turning her brand into a magazine and line of books.

Caitlin McNamara, Moxie & Oliver

www.moxieandoliver.com

Caitlin McNamara's creative business, Moxie & Oliver, was born in 2004 when Caitlin was stuck shopping for a black belt to fit her employer's dress code requirements. Unable to find a belt that she felt fit her personality and style, she headed to the local leather shop, bought some supplies and used her childhood memories of leather-working to create her own unique belt. She had so much fun that she made belts for all her friends and family that year for Christmas and began to sell her leather creations online part-time until she could afford to go full-time in 2010.

Jessica and Susan Partain, Inedible Jewelry

www.inediblejewelry.com

Sisters, Jessica and Susan Partain, started playing with polymer clay in their childhood and eventually began selling their miniature food charms locally at craft fairs. However, it wasn't until 2006 – when Jessica was finishing graduate school – that they began selling their creations online. Their products were such a hit that they were soon approached by a publisher at Random House, who asked them to write a Polymer Clay Cookbook with tutorials for a handful of their creations.

Heather Valentine, The Sewing Loft

www.thesewingloft.com

Designer and seamstress, Heather Valentine grew up watching her mother and grandmother repurpose and repair old clothes into new outfits and accessories. Those treasured life experiences and core values passed down from her family sparked her creativity and eventually led to the creation of her shop, The Sewing Loft, where Heather makes and sells patterns and upcycled creations made of repurposed felts, fabrics and other craft supplies.

Pam Walter, Kentucky Crafter's Corner

www.kycrafterscorner.com

When quilter, Pam Walter, moved to eastern Kentucky and started attending local arts and craft shows, she was shocked to discover that the artisans she met at fairs did not have their own websites or sell their products online. After serious consideration, she decided to create Kentucky Crafter's Corner to help other artists and crafters in her area market their works to a larger audience.

SUPPLY SOURCE DIRECTORY

AllArtSupplies.com
www.allartsupplies.com
Canvas, oil paints, acrylic paints, brush sets, chalk, charcoal, ceramic glazes, art frames, inks, sketch pencils, clay, drawing supplies, markers, crayons, oil pastels, tempera paint, origami, metal leafing, watercolor paints, screen printing, scratch art

Blick
www.dickblick.com
Illustrating, painting, air-brushing, ceramics, mosaics, print-making, scrapbooking, sculpture

CGW Enterprise
www.wholesaleyarnstore.com
Various yarns and knitting and crocheting tools

Clay King
www.clay-king.com
Pottery clay, pottery wheels, glazes, tools

Colonial Needle
www.colonialneedle.com
Crochet, needlepoint, knitting, felting

Craftster Shop
www.craftster.org/shop/craft-supplies
Clothing patterns, bag-making, jewelry and beading, knitting and crocheting, fabric, drawing, painting, inks, glass-working, pottery, leather, metal, wood, soap, candles, toys, dolls

Create for Less
www.createforless.com
Scrapbooking, sewing, beading, crochet, knitting

Darice
www.darice.com
Frames, beads, buttons, dolls, fabric, feathers, jewelry, magnet, macramé, paints, paper mache, metal, plaster, scrapbooking, sewing, yarn

Fabric Direct
www.fabricdirect.com
Fabric and upholstery

Factory Direct Craft
www.factorydirectcraft.com
Ornament-making, candle-making, doll-making, floral supplies, beading and jewelry-making, painting, soap-making

Fire Mountain Gems
www.firemountaingems.com
Beading, jewelry-making

Jo-Ann
www.joann.com
Fabric, quilting, scrapbooking, yarn, cross-stitch, beads, jewelry-making, ribbons, wood crafts, candle and soap-making, clay and t-shirts

Polymer Clay Express
www.polymerclayexpress.com
Polymer clay, tools and molds

Rio Grande
www.riogrande.com
Jewelry-making

Weaver Leather
www.leathersupply.com
Leather and leather working accessories and tools

Welding Depot
store.weldingdepot.com
Welding helmets, welding gear and guns, cutting equipment, metals

Wholesale Art Frames
www.wholesaleartframes.com
Frames, canvas, oil paints, easels, canvas stretchers, crayons, pencils, pastels

Wholesale Craft Outlet
www.ehobbycraft.com
Air-brushing, painting, clock-making, lamp-making, magnets, polymer clay, rubber stamping, sewing, scrapbooking

RESOURCE DIRECTORY

Productivity Tools

Pomodoro Technique
www.pomodorotechnique.com

Freedom
www.macfreedom.com

Self-Control
www.macupdate.com/app/mac/31289/selfcontrol

Harvest
www.getharvest.com

Legal Resources

Register Your Fictitious or "Doing Business As" (DBA) Name
www.sba.gov/content/register-your-fictitious-or-doing-business-dba-name

Registering Your Business at State Agencies
www.sba.gov/content/incorporating-your-business

S-Corporation Filing
www.irs.gov/instructions/i2553

Copyright Registration
www.copyright.gov

Online Patent Application
www.uspto.gov/patents

Online Trademark Application
www.uspto.gov/trademarks

Obtaining Business Licenses & Permits
www.sba.gov/content/obtaining-business-licenses-permits

Registering Your Business
www.sba.gov/content/5-steps-registering-your-business

Business Resources

Small Business Development Center
www.sba.gov/content/small-business-development-centers-sbdcs

Financial and Record-Keeping Resources

FreshBooks
www.freshbooks.com

Quicken
www.quicken.intuit.com

Outright
www.outright.com

Quick Books
quickbooks.intuit.com

Microsoft Excel
office.microsoft.com/en-us/excel

EverNote
www.evernote.com

Book: The Accounting Game
www.amazon.com/Accounting-Game-Basic-Fresh-
Lemonade/dp/1402211864

Small Business Administration: Record-Keeping
www.irs.gov/businesses/small/article/0,,id=98575,00.html

Tax Filing Resources

Turbo Tax
turbotax.intuit.com

Tax Act
www.taxact.com

Selling Online

Originl
www.originl.com

Etsy
www.etsy.com

Artfire
www.artfire.com

Dawanda
www.dawanda.com

Zibbet
www.zibbet.com

Shopify
www.shopify.com

Big Cartel
www.bigcartel.com

Big Commerce
www.bigcommerce.com

eBay
www.ebay.com

Webstore
www.webstore.com

OnlineAuction
www.onlineauction.com

Photo Editing Tools

Picnik
www.picnik.com

Picasa
picasa.google.com

Video Hosting Services

YouTube
www.youtube.com

Vimeo
www.vimeo.com

Website Building Tools/Services

WordPress
www.wordpress.com

SquareSpace
www.squarespace.com

Weebly
www.weebly.com

Domain Tools

Make Words
www.makewords.com

Marcaria
www.marcaria.com

Moniker
www.moniker.com

Name Boy
www.nameboy.com

Name Station
www.namestation.com

SEO Tools

Google's AdWords Keyword Analyzer
adwords.google.com/select/keywordtoolexternal

Google Analytics
analytics.google.com

Blogging Platforms

Originl
www.originl.com

WordPress
www.wordpress.com

Blogger
www.blogger.com

Tumblr
www.tumblr.com

Online Business Directories

Yahoo! Shopping
shopping.yahoo.com

Google Merchant Center
www.google.com/merchants

Google Places
www.google.com/places

Yahoo! Local Listings
listings.local.yahoo.com

CitySearch
www.citysearch.com

AOL's CityGuide
www.aolmedianetworks.com

MerchantCircle
www.merchantcircle.com

YellowPages
www.yellowpages.com

Creative Communities

Originl
www.originl.com

Craftser
www.craftster.org

Craft Juice
www.craftjuice.com

Get Crafty
www.getcrafty.com

Social Media

Facebook
www.facebook.com

Twitter
www.twitter.com

HootSuite
www.hootsuite.com

Social Bookmarking

StumbleUpon
www.stumbleupon.com

Pinterest
www.pinterest.com

Digg
www.digg.com

Reddit
www.reddit.com

Delicious
www.delicious.com

Promotional Items / Business Cards

Vistaprint
www.vistaprint.com

Moo
www.moo.com

Advertising

Google Adwords
adwords.google.com

Microsoft adCenter
advertising.microsoft.com/small-business

Craigslist
www.craigslist.com

Classifieds for Free
www.classifiedsforfree.com

Affiliates

ClickBank
www.clickbank.com

Commission Junction
www.cj.com

Payment Processing

PayPal
www.paypal.com

Square
www.squareup.com

Health Insurance Resources

Freelancer's Union
www.freelancersunion.org/benefits

Hiring Freelancers / Crowd-Sourcing Resources

oDesk
www.odesk.com

Elance
www.elance.com

Freelancer
www.freelancer.com

Squadhelp
www.squadhelp.com

Crowd Spring
www.crowdspring.com

REFERENCES

The Creative Mind

"Time" magazine: The Hidden Secrets of the Creative Mind
http://www.time.com/time/magazine/article/0,9171,1147152,00.html

Personal Empowerment: The Creative Mind – Learn Techniques for Engaging Your Creative Mind
http://www.affirmware.com.au/blog/engaging-creative-mind.html

Psychology Today: The Creative Personality
http://www.psychologytoday.com/articles/199607/the-creative-personality

The Daily Galaxy: Right Brain Smarts- Creative People's Brains Function Differently
http://www.dailygalaxy.com/my_weblog/2008/01/right-brain-sma.html

99% By Behance: Why Your Inner Critic Is Your Best Friend
http://the99percent.com/tips/6971/Why-Your-Inner-Critic-Is-Your-Best-Friend

Lateral Action: Is Everyone Creative?
http://lateralaction.com/articles/is-everyone-creative/

Being Your Own Boss

99% By Behance: It's Time to Kill Multi-Tasking
http://the99percent.com/articles/6986/Itas-Time-To-Kill-Multi-Tasking

Rena Tom: Prioritizing Work and Meeting Deadlines
http://renatom.net/2011/10/25/prioritizing-work-and-meeting-deadlines/

HomeBiz-Direct: Why Do So Many People Fail to Make Money Online?
http://www.homebiz-direct.com/blog/internet-marketing/why-do-so-many-people-fail-to-make-money-online/

SpyreStudios: The Benefits and Drawbacks of An Over-Active Creative Mind
http://spyrestudios.com/benefits-and-drawbacks-of-an-over-active-creative-mind/

Psychology Today: An In-House Retreat Can Refresh the Creative Mind
http://www.psychologytoday.com/blog/tracking-wonder/201011/in-house-retreat-can-refresh-the-creative-mind

99% By Behance: Don't Just Create "On Demand," Create For You
http://the99percent.com/tips/7050/Dont-Just-Create-On-Demand-Create-For-You

Building a Brand

Rena Tom: What's in a Name?
http://renatom.net/2011/11/01/whats-in-a-name/

Entrepreneur: How to Name Your Business
http://www.entrepreneur.com/article/21774

Working Solo: The Name Game – Naming Your Business
http://www.workingsolo.com/biztools/articles/naming.html

Small Business Administration: How to Name a Business
http://www.sba.gov/content/how-name-business

Strategic Planning for Creatives

Top Achievement: Creating S.M.A.R.T. Goals
http://topachievement.com/smart.html

Dummies.com: How to Establish Your Business's Vision, Mission and Values
http://www.dummies.com/how-to/content/how-to-establish-your-businesss-vision-mission-and.html

Inc.: How to Narrow Your Target Market
http://www.inc.com/guides/201104/how to narrow-your-target-market.html

The Right-Brain Business Plan: A Creative, Visual Map for Success
http://books.google.com/books/about/The_Right_Brain_Business_Plan.html?id=4hKACoL7jD0C

Legal Considerations

Rena Tom: I've got 99 problems, but the law ain't one
http://renatom.net/2011/10/24/ive-got-99-problems-but-the-law-aint-one/

The Crafts Report: Patent Protection for Your Craft
http://www.craftsreport.com/crafts-law/75-patentprotectionforyourcraft.html

Copyright: Copyright in General
http://copyright.gov/help/faq/faq-general.html

Creative Commons: About
http://creativecommons.org/about

Copyright: Registering a Work
http://www.copyright.gov/help/faq/faq-register.html

Plagiarism today: What is a Copyright?
http://www.plagiarismtoday.com/stopping-internet-plagiarism/your-copyrights-online/1-what-is-a-%20copyright/

WAHM.com: Starting a Craft Business- Copyrights and Intellectual Property
http://www.wahm.com/articles/starting-a-craft-business-copyrights-and-intellectual-property.html

InvestorGuide.com: What is an S Corporation?
http://www.investorguide.com/igu-article-1126-starting-your-business-what-is-an-s-corporation.html

IRS.gov: S Corporations
http://www.irs.gov/businesses/small/article/0,,id=98263,00.html

The Craft Artist's Legal Guide: Protect Your Work, Save on Taxes, Maximize Profits
http://books.google.com/books/about/The_Craft_Artist_s_Legal_G
uide.html?id=UoVX5q6O9bUC

Finances and Record-Keeping

Your Craft Business: Using a Record Keeping System for Your Craft Business
http://yourcraftbusiness.com/Your-Craft-Business/record-keeping-
craft-sales.htm

IRS: What Kind of Records Should I Keep?
http://www.irs.gov/businesses/small/article/0,,id=98551,00.html

Small Business Administration: Online Small Business Training
http://www.sba.gov/category/navigation-structure/counseling-
training/online-small-business-training

Accounting Coach: Introduction to Accounting Basics
http://www.accountingcoach.com/online-accounting-
course/60Xpg01.html

Pricing Your Creations

Direct Response.net: 2 Pricing Psychology Secrets Revealed
http://directresponse.net/2-pricing-psychology-secrets-revealed/

CBS: Pricing Psychology – 7 Sneaky Retail Tricks
http://www.cbsnews.com/8301-505144_162-41541822/pricing-
psychology-7-sneaky-retail-tricks/

Wise Bread: Party Like It's 19.99- The Psychology of Pricing
http://www.wisebread.com/party-like-its-1999-the-psychology-of-pricing

Selling Online

Big Cartel: Pricing and Sign Up
http://bigcartel.com/signup

eBay: Selling Basics – Quick Start Guide
http://pages.ebay.com/sellerinformation/howtosell/quickstartguide.html

Etsy: Fees
http://www.etsy.com/sell/fees

Art Fire: Sign Up Information
http://www.artfire.com/ext/referral/1/personalize

Dawanda: Fees
http://en.dawanda.com/info/page/service_fees

Online Selling Tips

The Etsy Blog: Best of the Etsy Forums – 20 Questions Your Buyers are Asking
http://www.etsy.com/blog/en/2010/best-of-the-etsy-forums-20-questions-your-buyers-are-asking/

The Etsy Blog: Seller How-To: 5 Tips for Item Descriptions
http://www.etsy.com/blog/en/2009/seller-how-to-5-tips-for-item-descriptions/

Tab Juice: Best Practices For Writing an Effective Product Description
http://www.tabjuice.com/scommerce-academy/best-practices-for-writing-an-effective-product-description/

Meylah: How to Write Winning Product Descriptions
http://meylah.com/meylah/how-to-write-winning-product-descriptions

Meylah: How to Write Product Descriptions That Tell a Story
http://meylah.com/meylah/how-to-write-product-description-that-tell-a-story

Marketing – Creating Demand

Business Opportunity Connection: The Difference Between Marketing and Selling
http://www.irepnetwork.com/blog/103/marketing-vs-selling/

Craft Zine: Why the Handmade Movement is Good for the American Economy
http://forums.craftzine.com/comments.php?DiscussionID=352

About.com: Marketing vs. Sales: What is the Difference?
http://marketing.about.com/cs/advertising/a/mrktingvssales.htm

Ten Online: Marketing Basics- What is Marketing?
http://tenonline.org/art/mm1/9301.html

Be Found Online

Fave Crafts: 10 Tips for Creating a Successful Craft Blog
http://www.favecrafts.com/Craft-Business/10-Tips-for-Creating-a-Successful-Craft-Blog

Online Networking

#socialmedia You Say?: #socialmedia – What Is It Good For?
http://www.socialmediayousay.com/2011/04/socialmedia-what-is-it-good-for.html

99% By Behance: It's Not About Engagement: Using Social Media to Make Ideas Happen
http://the99percent.com/tips/7048/Its-Not-About-Engagement-Using-Social-Media-To-Make-Ideas-Happen

Chris Brogan: 50 Ideas On Using Twitter For Business
http://www.chrisbrogan.com/50-ideas-on-using-twitter-for-business/

Promoting Your Business and Products Offline

FairsandFestivals.net: Writing a Press Release to Increase Your Art, Craft and Festival Business
http://www.fairsandfestivals.net/articles/view/writing-a-press-release-to-increase-your-art-craft-and-festival-business/

About.com: Selling Arts and Crafts on Consignment
http://artsandcrafts.about.com/od/consignmentsales/a/sellingoncons ignment.htm

Building Relationships with Buyers

About.com: Customer Relationships Are Key to Your Marketing Strategy
http://marketing.about.com/od/relationshipmarketing/a/crmstrategy. htm

Whale of a Blog: Forget Selling – Persuade Your Fans and Followers
http://www.whaleofablog.com/forget-selling-persuade-your-fans-followers/

Position 2: Stickiness – Convincing Your Brand's Fans and Followers to Stay
http://blogs.position2.com/stickiness-convincing-your-brands-fans-and-followers-to-stay

Advertising & Affiliates

PPC Campaigns: PPC or CPM – Which One Should You Go For?
http://www.perclickpays.com/perclickpays-articles/ppc-appraisal.php

Customer Service

Free Craft Fair: 6 Tips for Outstanding Craft Business Customer Service
http://freecraftfair.com/2010/12/6-tips-for-outstanding-craft-business-customer-service/

WAHM.com: 4 Tips to Provide Excellent Customer Service
http://freecraftfair.com/2010/12/6-tips-for-outstanding-craft-business-customer-service/

Taking the Next Step

CBS News: What is Crowdsourcing?
http://www.cbsnews.com/8301-505125_162-51052961/what-is-crowdsourcing/

Freelancers Union: Benefits 101
http://www.freelancersunion.org/benefits/benefits101.html

ABOUT THE AUTHOR

Doug Maxwell is a serial Internet entrepreneur with over 15 years of experience creating online businesses. A self-proclaimed creative, Doug has built a career creating web based software and successful businesses. His ventures include an online art gallery, web based career change assistance software and most recently the Originl creative community and selling platform. This unique blend of technology, design and career focus uniquely position Doug to assist creatives with entrepreneurial dreams. His love of art and design combined with the inspiration of family and friends remain a driving influence in these endeavors as well as this book.

INDEX

A SPECIAL INVITATION

We invite you to join us in the originl.com creative community. Discover the amazing creations our member community shares online or create your own portfolio site to showcase your work. Use the coupon code below to upgrade to a premium account and sell what you create with our integrated e-commerce platform to reach thousands of interested buyers.

---

60 Days Free Premium Membership

Code: **book60**

To redeem, sign up at: www.originl.com

3361487R00116

Printed in Great Britain
by Amazon.co.uk, Ltd.,
Marston Gate.